Photomontage

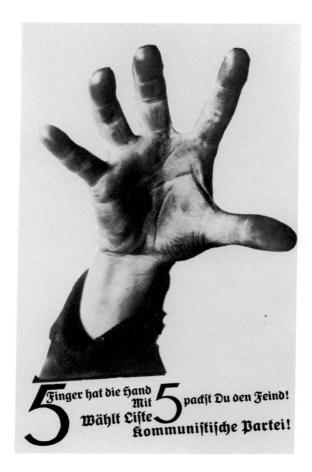

John Heartfield, *Fünf Finger hat die Hand. Mit fünf packst Du den Feind. Wählt Liste fünf kommunistische Partei!*
[The hand has five fingers. With five you seize the enemy. Vote List five Communist Party!]
1928

David Evans and Sylvia Gohl

Photomontage: a political weapon

Gordon Fraser · London

First published 1986 by
Gordon Fraser Gallery Ltd, London and Bedford
Copyright © David Evans and Sylvia Gohl 1986

British Library Cataloguing in Publication Data
Evans, David
    Photomontage: a political weapon.
    1. Heartfield, John
    I. Title   II Gohl, Sylvia
    770' .92'4   TR685
ISBN 0 86092 088 7
ISBN 0 86092 093 3 Pbk

Text set by August Filmsetting, Haydock, St Helens
Printed by The Roundwood Press Ltd, Kineton, Warwick
Bound by Hunter and Foulis Ltd, Edinburgh
Designed by Peter Guy

Contents

Acknowledgements

Introduction

Akademie der Künste der Deutschen Demokratischen Republik, John Heartfield-Archiv: 14 (lower), 15, 20, 21; Akademie der Künste der Deutschen Demokratischen Republik, John Heartfield-Archiv, Fotograph Bernd Kuhnert: 10 (upper), 14 (upper), 19, 28; Docklands Community Poster Project: 25 (upper); Edition Staeck: 10 (lower), 25 (lower), 29; Estate of George Grosz, Princeton, N.J.: 30; Peter Kennard: 24 (upper); The London Standard: 32; Novosti Press Agency: 23; The Royal Photographic Society, Bath: 11; Stichting de Wekker: 24 (lower); The Tate Gallery, London: 12

Plates

Akademie der Künste der Deutschen Demokratischen Republik, John Heartfield-Archiv, Fotograph Bernd Kuhnert: 38–70; Michael Bennett: 72–5; Carol Condé and Karl Beveridge: 76–7; Docklands Community Poster Project: 86–90; Edition Staeck: 85, 104–12; Peter Kennard: 92–101; David King: 102; Rhinoceros: 102–3; Stichting de Wekker: 78–84; Cath Tate: 113; Christer Themptander: 114–24, 128

Introduction

Two art scandals

In 1974 London's Institute of Contemporary Arts produced a show called 'Art into Society – Society into Art'. The contributors were all German artists interested in the social and political functions of their work. One of them was Klaus Staeck, well known in West Germany for his satirical photomontages. It was Staeck's work, especially the attacks on Bavaria's right-wing political boss Franz-Josef Strauss, which horrified some German officials who visited the show. Complaints to their government about the waste of taxpayers' money on political propaganda provoked a full-blown debate in the West German parliament and media about the freedom of artistic expression within a democracy.

In some ways the scandal was a storm in a teacup – all of Staeck's exhibits were widely available in West Germany as posters and postcards; the only official financial involvement with the show was help with the production of the catalogue by London's Goethe Institute, a cultural centre subsidised by the West German government. But the spectre of artistic censorship still shadows a country which has experienced repression under Nazism. Staeck and prestigious allies like the Nobel Prize winner Heinrich Böll, repeatedly stressed that the affair was symptomatic of a frightening drift towards a familiar authoritarianism.

Forty years earlier in 1934, the Mánes Art Association in Prague held a show of international caricature. It included thirty-six photomontages by the German artist John Heartfield who had fled to Czechoslovakia in 1933 when Hitler took power. His anglicised name (from Herzfelde) had been adopted as a protest against xenophobia during the First World War.

Hitler and Nazism were satirised in many of Heartfield's contributions to the exhibition and they provoked protests from the German ambassador in Prague. The Czech government responded to pressure from its more powerful neighbour and eventually the Mánes organisers were forced to remove seven montages including the one that had most offended the Nazis – a portrait of Hitler with a spinal column of gold coins and the title *Adolf the Superman: swallows gold and spouts junk*.

The censorship did not go unnoticed. As a result of local press coverage attendances at the exhibition rose and internationally-known

Heartfield, *On the intervention of the Third Reich. The more pictures they remove, the more visible the reality will be!*
See page 66

Staeck, *Bildersturm. Auf Eigentum kommt es hier nicht an*
[Iconoclasm. Private property rights do not matter in this case]
Subtitle: On 30 March 1976, CDU-CSU [Conservative] members of parliament tore posters off the walls and destroyed them during a Staeck exhibition in the Parliamentary Society building in Bonn.
1976

The posters on the floor are *Democracy needs to be bathed in blood on occasions* (Pinochet, Chile) and *25 years of human rights, 25 years of torture* (Amnesty International).

artists and intellectuals rallied to Heartfield's defence. Heartfield counter-attacked by producing postcards of some of the banned works and sending them to prominent Nazis. He also published a commemorative photomontage subtitled *The more pictures they remove, the more visible the reality will be!* (see pp. 9 and 66). In Czechoslovakia and abroad the scandal was seen as further evidence of the dictatorial, anti-democratic nature of Germany's new government.

The two scandals are separated by forty years, but closely related. Both revolve around artists who use photomontage – mainly a technique of combining different photographs to create a new message. Both artists use the technique to satirise the political establishment, and both are ready to counter-attack when the establishment expresses its displeasure. They are willing to use a gallery space when appropriate, but mainly concentrate on mass production and distribution outside the art world to ensure a wider, non-specialist audience.

The link between Heartfield and present-day artists like Staeck is the main theme of this essay, the first part of which examines Heartfield's distinctive development of photomontage in the twenties and thirties, and how far his ideas have influenced artists throughout the West. Later sections relate this body of work to photography, caricature and aesthetics.

From Dada to Productivism

The word *photomontage* means photo-construction or -assemblage. It was first used by the Berlin Dadaists – especially John Heartfield, George Grosz, Raoul Hausmann and Hannah Höch – to describe their experiments combining photographs from newspapers, magazines and so on. Precedents may be found in the composite pictures of many nineteenth-century photographers and in Cubist collage but the Dada context was new.

Dadaism was the first anti-art movement in history. Using tactics of shock, irony, protest, absurdity and violence, it aimed at demolishing a culture discredited by the Great War. The movement began in Zurich in 1916, but its impact was felt in New York, Paris, Cologne, Hanover and Berlin.

The extremist temper of the Berlin wing is illustrated by the exchange between the Dadaists Grosz and Heartfield and the painter

Oscar Rejlander, *Two Ways of Life*
1857

Oskar Kokoschka. After the Kapp Putsch of 1920 (an attempt by the radical right violently to overthrow the new Weimar Republic) clashes occurred between the army and workers in Dresden. A bullet went through the window of the Zwinger Gallery and damaged a Rubens painting. Incensed by the incident, Kokoschka — then art professor at the Dresden Academy — financed an appeal which appeared in local newspapers and as wallposters, urging the two sides to settle their scores well away from cultural treasures. Kokoschka's elevation of art above political struggle outraged Grosz and Heartfield who replied with a furious polemic 'Der Kunstlump' (The Artist as Scab) ridiculing the idea that art could be considered more important than the lives of workers. They welcomed the fact that bullets had penetrated galleries, palaces and a Rubens, rather than the homes of the poor.

The visual equivalent of their cultural nihilism was photomontage —

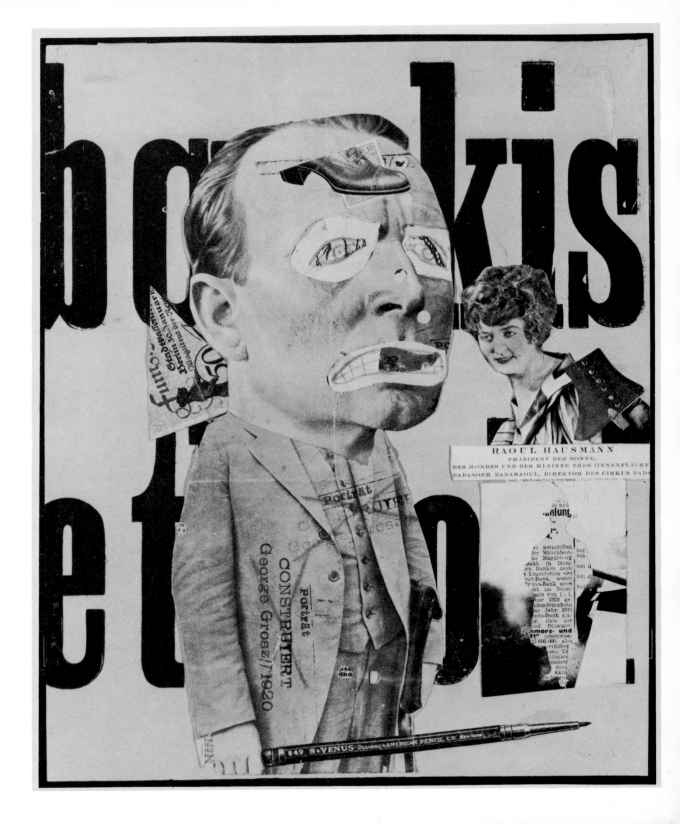

a stab in the eye of good taste. More specifically, the technique was part of the Berlin Dada revolt against the pervasive influence of Expressionism. The latter had been the first example of modern art in Germany, and was particularly associated with the pre-war *Brücke* and *Blaue Reiter* groups. For Expressionists, the imitation of nature which had been the post-Renaissance artist's main preoccupation had become irrelevant with the invention of the camera. Therefore, the new aim of the artist had to be the depiction of inner states which were outside the camera's domain. 'I have no fear of photography as long as it cannot be used in heaven and hell', asserted the Norwegian artist Edvard Munch, a major inspiration for German Expressionists. But for the Dadaists, photomontage's mechanical, impersonal qualities offered a powerful antidote to what they considered Expressionist self-indulgence.

Heartfield, Grosz and the other Dadaists had all been profoundly touched by Expressionism which had not been just a new art movement but a form of messianic revolt, and had inspired widespread pacifism in the Great War. But by the close of the war, the changing political situation, above all the Russian Revolution in 1917, had made Expressionism irrelevant. Later Heartfield assessed Dadaism thus: 'The greatest significance of Dadaism was that it immunised us against relapsing into Expressionism, which had lost its original importance as a result of the new political situation.'

Heartfield was an early member of the German Communist Party, joining on the last day of 1918 with his brother Wieland Herzfelde and George Grosz. The Communist Party viewed their Dada experiments with scepticism; its official newspaper condemned the polemic against Kokoschka as 'true vandalism'. But Berlin Dada was, in any case, coming to an end. Its climax was the notorious Dada Fair of 1920, which resulted in court appearances for some of the participants for insulting the German army. Meanwhile Heartfield tried new ways of serving the Communist cause more directly.

A focus for much of this work was Wieland Herzfelde's gallery and publishing house, Malik Verlag. The firm's early history clearly registers all the transformations outlined above. Founded in 1916, its first publication was an anti-war magazine called *Neue Jugend* (New Youth), deeply imbued with Expressionism. Immediately after the Great War it became a major outlet for Dada publications, including the catalogue of the 1920 Dada Fair. Then, in the twenties and thirties,

Raoul Hausmann, *The Critic*
1919

Heartfield, *After ten years: fathers and sons 1924*
See pages 40–1

George Grosz and John Heartfield,
Dada-merika
1919

it became an unofficial outlet for Communist art and ideas, often using Heartfield's pioneering photomontage dustjackets.

In 1924 Heartfield became secretary of the newly formed 'Red Group' of Communist artists, committed to the development of revolutionary propaganda. Shortly afterwards, he produced a photomontage which was the prototype of a new political art. Called *After ten years: fathers and sons 1924*, it was made to commemorate the tenth anniversary of the outbreak of the Great War. In it, young cadets are led by a German general, overlooked by the skeletons of their fathers who had fallen in combat. The image recalled the Great War and also warned against the re-emergence of a dangerous militarism which might lead to another. (Ominously, the German war hero General von Hindenburg was elected President of the Republic in the following year.) The montage was enlarged and displayed in the window of the Malik bookshop, surrounded by various war mementoes. The display aroused great public interest and curious crowds had to be dispersed by police.

A comparison of *After ten years* with Grosz and Heartfield's *Dada-merika* (1919) illustrates the break in Heartfield's approach to photomontage. The Dada work is an almost random mixture of printed ephemera, deliberately *lacking* all the attributes of a traditional easel painting: controlled composition, perspective, precise subject matter. But in his later work all three features are re-introduced.

Both photomontages employ photographic source material, but for entirely different reasons. *Dada-merika*, in common with most Dada photomontages, uses photographs from newspapers and magazines to insult painters and their audiences, who are committed to art as personal creativity. In the post-Dada work, photography is used because it is the most accessible visual medium for a non-specialist mass audience.

There is a parallel change in the use made of text. In the Dada montage words are integrated into the image to lampoon the conventional separation of a painting and its title. In the later work, a title is introduced to clarify the meaning of the image.

The Berlin Dadaists tried to demolish easel painting with photomontage. Their methods were outrageous but in their creation of unique images they were reproducing an important feature of the art they opposed and allowing subsequent speculation in Dada commodities. Heartfield solved this problem by continually experimenting with

Heartfield, cover for Kurt Tucholsky's book,
Deutschland, Deutschland über Alles,
Neuer Deutscher Verlag, 1929

various forms of mass production and distribution. In the twenties he 'made the book jacket into a political instrument' (Walter Benjamin, 1934). He also designed posters, magazines, newspapers, calendars, pamphlets and, with the writer Kurt Tucholsky, produced *Deutschland, Deutschland über Alles* (1929), a new kind of satirical photo-text book. In short he deliberately broke down the traditional distinction between fine and applied arts.

His attempts to develop a form of revolutionary graphics based on photomontage were closely related to a Soviet movement called Productivism. In 1924 one of its main theoreticians, Boris Arvatov, defined 'production art' as 'those types of utilitarian-reproductive art which have a mass character, are executed by means of technology and are in close contact with the material, everyday life of the urban industrial worker'. He cited as examples posters, illustrations, advertisements, film and photography. Photography was particularly useful because the photographer captured life and events more cheaply, quickly and precisely than the painter. In 1928 Arvatov was a founder member of the October Group, committed to integrating art and production. Members of the photography section of the October Group were obliged to become press photographers and to attach themselves to a factory or commune, because, according to the section's programme of 1930, 'only concrete participation in production guarantees to the photoworker the social meaning of his work'.

Heartfield was well informed about Productivism. He cooperated with the October Group's secretary A. I. Gutnov who organised an exhibition of their work in Berlin in 1930. The following year he visited the Soviet Union, and became involved in several Productivist projects. He worked on two issues of *The USSR in Construction*, an illustrated magazine which appeared in five languages. He produced a Lenin montage for the magazine's cover which was later converted into a monumental mural in a Moscow street as well as being used as a stage projection in a Moscow theatre. In response to the Productivist demand for the 'democratisation' of artistic technique he organised photomontage workshops for Red Army officers and students.

Heartfield's guide to the Soviet Union was the writer and critic Sergei Tretyakov (later to write the first book on Heartfield, published in Moscow in 1936). In the late twenties and early thirties he acted as an informal cultural diplomat, disseminating the latest Soviet ideas in Germany and bringing German ideas back to the Soviet Union. During Heartfield's Soviet visit, Tretyakov introduced him to the artists Rodchenko and El Lissitzky, both of whom had abandoned painting for photography and photomontage.

There is a close link between Tretyakov's ideas about revolutionary art – described variously as Productivism, Factography or Operationalism – and Heartfield's mature work. In literature, Tretyakov stressed the irrelevance of the nineteenth-century Realist novel with its emphasis on the individual hero, plot and characterisation. Instead he advocated a literature of facts, tackling subjects like wood, bread, coal, iron or the locomotive. As a model he presented his own *Feld-Herren* (The Generals), published in Germany by Herzfelde's Malik Verlag, whose main theme was the Soviet collectivisation of agriculture. Typically, the book was produced with the active collaboration of agricultural workers. In the visual arts, Tretyakov was enthusiastic about the possibilities of the camera for accurately recording the Soviet experiment.

He was confident that journalism, written or photographic, could be mastered by any Soviet citizen and urged the creation of worker-correspondents who would eventually eliminate outmoded, individualistic art forms. For Tretyakov, 'Each boy with his camera is a soldier in the war against easel painters, and each little reporter is stabbing *belles-lettres* to death with the point of his pen.' He was impatient with those who were waiting for the 'red Tolstoy' and insisted that the Soviet Union already had its own 'collective Tolstoy' in the newspapers.

Montage of all kinds played an important role in Tretyakov's theory, because it was the device which distinguished a mere reporter from an 'operational artist'. In writing, this meant converting a collection of facts into a significant message about reality by intelligent editing. In photography, the individual image was no more than 'an infinitely fine scale that has been scratched from the surface of reality with the fingernail'. However, an isolated shot could contribute to a valuable statement about the world as part of a photo-series, such as Rodchenko's two-year project on the construction of the White Sea canal, or in a photomontage.

Tretyakov described Heartfield as the main Bolshevik artist in Germany. He earned this title with his Malik Verlag book covers, but above all with the new kind of planned photo-reportage which he developed in the thirties.

Agit-Prop

In 1930 a small note appeared in a German illustrated magazine informing the readership that John Heartfield was going to be a regular contributor. The magazine – *Arbeiter-Illustrierte-Zeitung* (Workers' Illustrated Paper) or *A-I-Z* – subsequently published over two hundred of his photomontages. This body of work, the core of Heartfield's artistic achievement, remains one of the few instances of twentieth-

A-I-Z cover
1932

century avant-garde art outside the Soviet Union which aimed at, and reached, a mass audience.

A-I-Z was founded in Berlin in 1925 and switched to Prague when Hitler took power in Germany in 1933 (when the abbreviation became *AIZ*). In 1936 it changed its name to *Die Volks-Illustrierte* (The People's Illustrated), and it collapsed in 1938, shortly before the Nazi invasion of Czechoslovakia. The magazine was Communist, but never an official organ of the German Communist Party. Designed mainly for German workers, its continual theme was the contrast between a world to conquer – capitalism – and a world to defend – the Soviet Union.

The imaginative use of photographs differentiated *AIZ* from most other revolutionary newspapers and magazines, with the possible exception of *The USSR in Construction*, whose contributors included outstanding artists like El Lissitzky and Rodchenko. This was no accident: *AIZ*'s founder, Willi Münzenberg, modelled his new magazine on the illustrated magazines that flourished in Germany in the twenties such as the *Berliner Illustrirte Zeitung, Kölnische Illustrierte* and the *Münchner Illustrierte Presse*. These all contained fresh styles of photo-journalism, made possible by innovations in photographic technology: the small lightweight cameras like the Leica which gave photographers a new flexibility; 35mm perforated film which made possible sequential photography and photo-stories; wide-aperture lenses which allowed photographers to work in previously impossible light conditions.

Münzenberg wanted to match the photographic dynamism of the establishment illustrated magazines, but for a different end – to show in pictures all aspects of working-class life. To generate this material he tried to encourage readers who were amateur photographers to become class-conscious photo-correspondents, paralleling the initiatives of the Soviet Productivists. A worker-photographer group was set up in Hamburg in 1926 and by the early thirties similar groups were active throughout Germany and abroad, including England and the United States. The German movement even had its own magazine *Der Arbeiter-Fotograf* (The Worker-Photographer) which sought to encourage good technique and Socialist ways of seeing. The experiment was brought to an end however, by Hitler's takeover in 1933. Exiled to Prague, *AIZ* was increasingly forced to rely on the clever editing of photographs from conventional picture agencies, and probably this contributed to a greater dependence on photomontage.

Heartfield also escaped to Prague in 1933, and continued to supply photomontages to *AIZ*. Indeed he became more involved with the magazine and was, for a time, its editor. He was regularly given a page and often the front or back cover to comment on topical events. Obviously his key themes were attacks on Nazism and defence of the Soviet Union.

In 1931 in Moscow he described his aims:

> If I collect documents, combine them and do that in a clever way, then the agitational-propagandistic effect on the masses will be immense. And that is the most important thing for us. That is the foundation of our work. Therefore, it is our task to influence the masses, as well, as strongly, as intensely as possible.

Thus each photomontage aimed to be both agitational – encouraging a Communist response to particular events – and propagandist – trying to develop in the viewer an overall Communist understanding of the world. In short Heartfield wanted to develop Marxist-Leninist agit-prop.

The aim was the creation of good Communists, the tactic – shock. Not shock in a Dadaist sense however – by the thirties Heartfield was no longer interested in Dada's violent, but often diffuse, attacks on bourgeois philistinism. Heartfield's shock effects also differed from Surrealist attempts to jolt the unconscious – Max Ernst's collages, for example. The closest parallel was probably the *Verfremdungseffekt* (estrangement effect) in Brecht's epic theatre. In their respective fields both Heartfield and Brecht sought to present the familiar in an unfamiliar way, to encourage in working people new political insight and activity. Two examples involving well-known paintings reveal the range of shock or estrangement effects in Heartfield's work.

War (*AIZ* 1933) was subtitled *A painting by Franz v. Stuck. Brought up to date by John Heartfield*. Von Stuck's original was a celebration of Nordic warrior values, showing a young naked rider crossing a battlefield of corpses. Heartfield's additions – the swastika-shaped lightning, the gas mask on a corpse, Hitler sitting uncomfortably behind the young warrior – created a simple effect but a complex message. On one level, it was a warning about Nazi militarism, a visual representation of the German Communist leader Ernst Thälmann's remark 'Hitler – that's war'. On another level, it was satirising Nazi

Heartfield, *War*
See pages 54–5

SOWJETAUFBAU UND NAZIAUFBAU

Die Sowjetunion ist eine der größten Industriemächte der Welt geworden

Die Sammelaktionen haben riesenhafte Ausmaße angenommen

Heartfield, *Sowjetaufbau und Naziaufbau*
[Soviet construction and Nazi construction]
AIZ, 1934

aesthetics. Von Stuck's painting was a typical example of the mythical art and values Hitler tried to promote whilst attacking the products of Modernism, including Heartfield's work, as 'degenerate'.

Liberty herself fights in their ranks (*Volks-Illustrierte* 1936) combined Delacroix's celebration of the French Revolution of 1830 with a press photograph of Republicans defending Madrid during the Spanish Civil War. The result (page 69) was an inspirational montage, a morale booster to remind the oppressed of history's liberating moments.

Both montages require the viewer to recognise the paintings or at least the styles of painting and then to oscillate between their original meanings and their new meanings in a changed context. In each case, the familiar was made unfamiliar, but in the first example the effect was satirical and in the second, heroic. Heartfield experimented with both approaches. Sometimes the two were combined, as in *Soviet construction and Nazi construction* (*AIZ* 1934) which plays on the formal similarities between a photograph of Soviet industrialisation and a pile of collection boxes for a Nazi charity. But in general the two were kept separate. Anti-Nazi montages, the bulk of his work in the thirties, tended to be satirical and made use of a biting humour to analyse, attack, warn. Heroic montages were much rarer, mainly celebrating the Soviet Union as a lighthouse of progress in a sea of barbarism.

Heartfield was an artist, not a political thinker. None of his principal themes such as Hitler as a militarist or a puppet of big business, would have surprised regular readers of *AIZ*. His genius was to translate current Communist ideas into striking visual images.

By 1930 Heartfield had a formidable range of montage techniques at his disposal. Sometimes the montage effect involved the juxtaposition of a single photograph with text, sometimes the juxtaposition of two photographs. Occasionally he constructed and photographed an object in the studio: a technique closely related to Dada and Surrealist transformations of everyday materials. But above all his photomontages were assemblages of different photographic fragments. Usually this involved printing, cutting up and pasting together different images, followed by some retouching, but he also sandwiched negatives together in the enlarger and produced a montage on a single sheet of photographic paper. Compare the plates on pages 50, 59, 68.

Reflecting on photomontage in 1931, Hausmann wrote of 'static film' and Heartfield saw his role as analogous to that of a film director. Not only was the montage of photographs and texts equivalent to film

and drawing.' Staeck, in particular, has developed the photo-text
montage, often mimicking commercial advertising with his juxtaposition of a single glossy photograph and a witty, contradictory caption.
On occasions he has abandoned photography altogether, creating a
montage by combining dissonant texts.

Heartfield's exploration of estrangement effects has been especially
influential. The device is regularly used by Peter Kennard to 'break
open the surface of deceit and show the conflicts that go on under-
neath'. By subverting the visually commonplace – a Constable painting
(pages 92–3), a tourist postcard, a map of Britain, the globe – his best
and most recent work invites the viewer, in John Berger's phrase, 'to
see through (the popular expression is very apt) the lie.'

Photography

The basic element of every photomontage is the photograph.

Heartfield's development of photomontage during the twenties co-
incided with a period of innovation for German photography, largely
fuelled by the ceaseless demand for novelty in photojournalism and
advertising. The *Film und Foto* exhibition, presented by the Deutsche

Werkbund in Stuttgart in 1929, drew attention to these innovations. Over one thousand photographs were displayed in thirteen galleries. The perspective was international, with distinguished photographers responsible for choosing photographs to represent different countries. Edward Steichen and Edward Weston made the American selection, El Lissitzky the Soviet and László Moholy-Nagy the German. As well as the official catalogue, two books were published in Germany to complement the exhibition: Werner Gräff's *Es kommt der neue Fotograf!* (Here Comes the New Photographer!) and *foto-auge* (photo-eye) by Franz Roh and Jan Tschichold. Heartfield was featured in both books and in the exhibition, though he never associated himself with the movement known as 'New Photography'.

'New Photographers' were preoccupied with developing a photographic art free from painterly assumptions. 'Certain rules that stem from bygone eras of painting are set up as iron laws. They can easily be shown to be untenable', asserted Werner Gräff briskly in his preface. Franz Roh's introduction to *foto-auge* condemned attempts 'to imitate the charm that belongs either to painting or to graphic art' as 'a deviation from the proper task of photography'. Albert Renger-Patzsch, perhaps the best-known 'New Photographer', summarised the approach with his demand for 'photographic photography'.

For Renger-Patzsch, photography's terrain was easy to define. Its subject matter was the natural and man-made world, an area which, because of the camera's greater speed, precision and objectivity, could no longer be monopolised by the traditional visual arts. Its special tools were light, camera, darkroom and the photographer's eye and taste. Its distinctive aim was not to imitate painting, but to encourage people to view their environment with fresh eyes.

A link between 'New Photography' and Heartfield was provided by the critic Walter Benjamin. Benjamin admired some of the new developments. He favourably reviewed Karl Blossfeldt's *Urformen der Kunst* (The Prototypes of Art, 1928) which contained photographs of plants, enlarged to colossal size. Here the camera was in its own domain, improving on the naked eye to reveal 'an unexpected wealth of forms and analogies which we never imagined existed in the plant world'. He also praised August Sander's use of the camera to compile a visual inventory of social types in *Antlitz der Zeit* (Countenance of the Time, 1929). Both projects were admired by Benjamin because they demonstrated the camera's power as a tool for scientific or sociological classification. His contempt was reserved for attempts to develop photography as an art form, typified by Renger-Patzsch.

Renger-Patzsch's *Die Welt.ist schön* (The World is beautiful, 1928) was the most famous example of 'New Photography', consisting of one hundred plates, divided into sections such as plants, animals, material and architecture. Mundane domestic or industrial objects were often chosen as subject matter. (He originally wanted to call the book *Things*.) These were presented in unusual ways using a variety of devices such as radical cutting, close up, sharp contrast, dramatic use of diagonals and surprising perspectives. Benjamin's view of the book and the photography it exemplified was scathing: *'The world is beautiful* — that is its motto. Therein is unmasked the posture of a photography that can endow any soup can with cosmic significance but cannot grasp a single one of the human connections in which it exists...'

Benjamin was aware of the commercial applications of Renger-Patzsch's approach. These were emphasised in the introduction to *Die Welt ist schön* and amongst the plates was the pioneering advertising photograph for Hag coffee, showing the beans spilling out of a packet next to a fresh cup of black coffee. But against such attempts to 'charm and persuade' Benjamin advocated a photography which sought to 'experiment and instruct'. Within Germany, Heartfield represented this alternative to Renger-Patzsch.

Like the 'New Photographers', Heartfield wanted to encourage 'seeing', but through proletarian eyes. In his attempts to heighten class consciousness through the experimental, didactic use of photomontage he relied on and manipulated two categories of popular knowledge: firstly, knowledge of the reality depicted in photographs and secondly, knowledge of the medium of photography.

The success of Heartfield's works depended on the popular awareness of figures, images and situations which, in themselves, had nothing specifically to do with photography. One of the world's oldest religious symbols, the swastika, was closely linked with the revival of Germanic ideas at the end of the nineteenth century. In 1935 it was adopted as Nazi Germany's official symbol and permeated every aspect of German life until the defeat of Nazism in 1945. By the thirties, every German would have recognised the swastika as a symbol of Nazism and its 'New Order'. Every German would have also understood Heartfield's intended 'dis-order' when, for example, he created a swastika from crossed bloody axes (page 58).

Heartfield, *Millions stand behind me!*
See page 49

Heartfield, *Don't worry – he's a vegetarian!*
See page 55

FACING PAGE ABOVE
Staeck, *Das Neue PAL*
Subtitle: slaughter-fresh from the can.
1969

FACING PAGE BELOW
Staeck, *Entmannt alle Wüstlinge, Wählt christlich*
[Castrate all libertines. Vote Christian]
1972

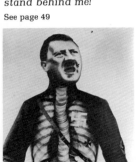

Heartfield, *Adolf – the Superman*
See page 48

Kennard, *Falklands medal*
See page 98

Kennard, *Maggie Regina*
See page 99

On one level, Heartfield's photomontages worked by disrupting popular assumptions about the everyday reality shown in photographs. But they also worked on levels more specifically photographic. They had a 'parasitical' relationship with the rules of scale and perspective. Some gained their effects by appearing to obey the rules, others by openly flaunting them. An instance of the former was Heartfield's blending of the features of Kaiser Wilhelm and Adolf Hitler. The artist's sensitivity towards popular perceptions of scale, combined with an awareness of 'correct' lighting and a cunning disguise of joins, created the impression of a conventional studio portrait, at first glance. An example of the latter was Heartfield's best-known montage *Millions stand behind me*. The gigantic size of the left-hand figure in relation to Hitler instantly ruled out the possibility that this was a documentary photograph. The viewer was forced to recognise a photomontage which used the device of exaggerated scale to suggest that Hitler was merely a stooge of big business. These distinctions were poles of orientation rather than rigid categories, because Heartfield frequently combined the two approaches in a single work. *Don't worry, he's a vegetarian* preserved the perspective of an ordinary studio photograph, but a variety of unrealistic details (the awkward position of Hitler's head, the Gallic cock's liberty bonnet) encouraged the viewer to recognise a photomontage.

Heartfield also exploited popular knowledge about varieties of photography, normally recognised as different territories with specific subject matter and presentation. *Adolf – the Superman* daringly combined press and scientific photography to make a point. By using an X-ray photograph he invited the viewer to 'see through' the press image. Here science revealed what was normally absent in establishment press photographs of Hitler: his financial backing.

Similar distinctions can be applied to more recent photomontage. Artists still exploit non-photographic knowledge, especially of political symbols and the features of political leaders. They continue to play with scale and perspective. Kennard's blending of Margaret Thatcher and Queen Victoria, like Heartfield's *His Majesty Adolf*, gains its effect by appearing initially to be a conventional studio portrait. But usually he goes to the other extreme, creating a message by audaciously disrupting popular perceptions of photography. For example, his comment on the recent Falklands War involves confusing the scale of a medal and an exploding warship. There is also continued interest in

yoking together different types of photography. The juxtaposition of commercial and press genres is a common device. In Staeck's *New PAL* a colour advertisement for dog food is placed upon black and white coarsely screened press photographs of a young famine victim. Staeck's indictment of North/South disparities depends on the viewer recognising the press photographs as the 'real' against which the advertisement is assessed.

In one respect however, there is a significant difference between the work of Heartfield and present-day artists. The latter have Heartfield's work as a frame of reference. Part of the effect of Staeck's *Castrate all libertines* depends on recognising the allusion to Heartfield's *Don't worry, he's a vegetarian*. Similarly, Dunn and Leeson's *Passing the Buck* (page 90), in terms of image and the title's wordplay, recalls Heartfield's *Millions stand behind me*.

Overall, present-day artists share Heartfield's ambiguous attitude towards photography. They are willing to take advantage of the eye-witness reputation of a photograph, but are sceptical about the power of an isolated image. Photomontage provides a way out. With photomontage they can squeeze extra meaning from photographs by disrespectfully separating and re-combining the various levels in different photographic fragments. These transgressions are not ends in themselves; they are attempts to meet Benjamin's demand for a photography that combines experimentation and instruction.

Political Cartoons

As well as fine art, agit-prop and photography, the tradition of modern political cartooning is important to photomontage. Satirical photomontage could be defined as the continuation of political cartooning by other means.

Heartfield has a complex relationship with George Grosz, perhaps the greatest satirical cartoonist of the Weimar period. Their friendship began in 1915, when both were fiercely pacifist. They were key figures in the Berlin Dada movement, often co-producing photomontages (a further way of subverting the idea of individual artistic creativity). Both joined the Communist Party and, in the twenties, sought to develop a committed art to serve the revolutionary cause. In 1919, with Heartfield's brother, Wieland Herzfelde, they published the first

George Grosz, *Früh um fünf Uhr*
[Five a.m.]

Das Gesicht der herrschenden Klasse, Malik Verlag, 1921

German Communist satirical magazine *Die Pleite* (Bankruptcy) which included line cartoons by Grosz and Heartfield. Together they wrote the anti-Kokoschka polemic 'Der Kunstlump', published in 1920, and both held posts in the various Communist organisations of artists like the Red Group of 1924. The main outlet for Grosz's books and portfolios of satirical cartoons was Herzfelde's publishing house Malik Verlag. *Das Gesicht der herrschenden Klasse* (The Face of the Ruling Class), for instance, was published by Herzfelde in 1921 and was one of the first examples of a Marxist-Leninist picture book designed to encourage revolutionary class consciousness. The book relied heavily on tendentious juxtaposition within and between cartoons. Grosz also included one photomontage *Hohenzollern Renaissance*, superimposing the heads of famous politicians onto a painting of the royal family. Typically Grosz signed the work with a rubber stamp. Another distinctive feature, recalling the graphic work of Goya and Daumier, was the frequent use of ironic captions drawn from popular sources like songs, proverbs and the Bible. All of these elements were extended in Heartfield's photomontages for *AIZ* a decade later.

Both Grosz and Heartfield shared a fascination for the French caricaturist Honoré Daumier (1808–79). They developed a first-hand knowledge of his work through their mutual friend Eduard Fuchs, the cultural historian, who had accumulated the largest Daumier collection in Europe. Heartfield wrote two articles on Daumier, published in 1937 and 1942. In both pieces Heartfield praised Daumier as an engaged artist, who used caricature to support Republicanism against the tyrannies of the Orléanist Louis Philippe and the Bonapartist Napoleon III. For Heartfield, Daumier's work was an inspiration in the struggle against the twentieth-century tyranny of Fascism.

The history and theory of the modern political cartoon has been usefully analysed by the art historians Ernst Kris and E. H. Gombrich and their ideas are directly relevant to understanding satirical photomontage. Both Kris and Gombrich stressed the relative novelty of the medium, which probably began in England in the eighteenth century when comic artists such as James Gillray produced visual satires combining two distinct traditions of representation. On the one hand, they contained symbolic personification, as old as Ancient Greek and Roman mythology; on the other hand, the 'loaded portrait' or *caricatura* associated with the Italian Annibale Carracci (1560–1609). Both aspects are detectable in Heartfield's photomontages. 'Justice' and

'Liberty' as female figures were obvious symbolic personifications while 'loaded portraits' of Nazi leaders were his most famous images.

In his lecture 'The Cartoonist's Armoury' (1962), Gombrich examined some of the main weapons of political cartoonists. He gave particular prominence to the visualisation of figures of speech, as in Daumier's depiction of the 'balance of power' with Europe personified by a frightened woman, balancing uneasily on a smoking bomb. Heartfield used this device frequently. Hitler as a 'puppet', Goering 'playing with fire' and the Third Reich as a 'house of cards' (page 51) were all making metaphoric language visible.

Gombrich also considered the portrait caricature which 'gave the artist the means of turning an intellectual equation into a visual fusion'. His example was Gillray's cartoon of the eighteenth-century Whig politician Charles James Fox dressed as a *sans-culotte*. The face was a 'loaded portrait', but the real novelty was the composite figure, making a visual link between a British political party and the radical movement of the French Revolution. One of Heartfield's main achievements was a continuation of this tradition, bringing together the apparently incongruous to convey visually the Communist view of the Nazis as, for example, pawns of big business or militarists.

Gombrich examined the 'political bestiary' and suggested that the 'cartoonist's zoo' drew, first, on the fable traditions of Aesop and La Fontaine which attached human meanings to certain animals, and secondly on the tradition of heraldic beasts used on coats of arms and as national emblems. Heartfield, like his hero Daumier, regularly exploited popular knowledge of fables. Peace was a dove, threatened by Nazi foxes, hawks, snakes, toads, vultures, wolves and predatory fish. Less frequently he drew on the heraldic tradition, for example, representing France as the Gallic cock with liberty bonnet.

Gombrich's remarks on natural metaphors, such as the contrast between light and dark representing the conflict between good and evil, also provide an insight into Heartfield's work. His photomontage about the Nazi book burnings, *Through Light into the Night*, created its effect by ironically reversing the normal associations of light and enlightenment (page 59).

Finally Gombrich stressed the power of contrast, especially the contrast of scales, used for satirical effect in a literary context by Jonathan Swift in *Gulliver's Travels*. This device was regularly employed by Heartfield, most famously in *Millions stand behind me* (page 49).

Figures of speech, portrait caricature, the political bestiary, natural metaphors and the power of contrast are five features linking traditional political cartoonists with the Heartfield tradition of photomontage. A further link is an interest in the latest methods of mass reproduction of images. Daumier worked with lithography and Heartfield designed for new developments in photogravure, which *AIZ* used to achieve high-quality photographic reproduction. One recent development in photomontage has been the exploration (particularly by Klaus Staeck) of full-colour offset lithography.

Mass production opens the possibility of mass influence – one reason why radical political cartoonists have been threatened by censorship. Political cartoonists such as Daumier and Grosz and artists in the Heartfield tradition have frequently been prosecuted by the authorities; Heartfield was regularly taken to court even before the Nazis took power and Staeck's photomontages have to date already provoked some forty court cases.

One of the distinctive achievements of Heartfield and his followers has been to merge twentieth-century techniques of photomontage with the older tradition of political cartooning to create a special type of visual satire. Often the basic idea of a photomontage and a more conventionally produced cartoon are similar – the anti-Nazi messages of Heartfield and the cartoonist David Low frequently overlapped – but the montage artist's use of photographs conveys an enhanced sense of the 'real' which increases the power of the message. The photograph's potential caused Grosz to be disparaging about his own achievements as a visual propagandist in the twenties: 'The time of the caricature as an instrument in the struggle for freedom and progress was long past: if people were to be aroused nowadays, then the trick was best done with photographs and suitable captions.'

David Low, *House of Cards*
Evening Standard, 25 August 1944

Revolutionary Aesthetics

In his essay 'The Political Uses of Photo-Montage' (1969) John Berger assessed Heartfield. For Berger, Heartfield showed genius when he used photomontage to demystify things, and Berger suggested that this possibility should be further explored by future montage artists. For him, the least useful aspect of Heartfield's work was the occasional tendency to slip into a simplified moral exhortation.

Present-day montage artists are aware of the technique's weaknesses. The Swedish photomonteur Christer Themptander has warned against a visual rhetoric which ends discussion rather than starts one. Klaus Staeck recently criticised some of his own work for using exhausted symbolism which no longer stimulates thought. He gave as an example the use of a bowler hat, glass of champagne and paunch to signify 'boss' at a time when German employers are obsessed with fitness training.

The most influential *rejection* of photomontage as a whole came from the Marxist critic Georg Lukács. His views emerged in the late thirties in an urgent debate amongst contributors to *Das Wort*, a Moscow-based German literary magazine that provided a forum for anti-Fascist writers and critics in exile. Lukács' polemics about the cultural roots of Fascism were written in the thirties but had a long life, frequently being adapted to legitimise Soviet attacks on Modernists (including Heartfield) in the name of Socialist Realism.

Lukács conceded that photomontage could have the effect of a good joke and even, on occasions, become a powerful political weapon. However, photomontage was generally incapable of making any significant statement about the world because its basic element, the photograph, could only record surface appearances and reveal nothing of society's hidden mechanisms. Consequently, within a photomontage, 'The details may be dazzlingly colourful in their diversity, but the whole will never be more than an unrelieved grey on grey. After all, a puddle can never be more than dirty water, even though it may contain rainbow tints.'

Lukács offered no evidence to support these dismissive remarks and had no particular interest in photomontage or the visual arts. His specialist area was literature and the comments on photomontage were asides in what was primarily an attack on certain literary Modernists for whom montage was a major principle. In Tretyakov's writings, Döblin's novel *Berlin Alexanderplatz* (1929) or the Brecht-Weill opera *Rise and Fall of the City Mahagonny* (1930), dissimilar materials were deliberately connected. Lukács regarded this scissors-and-paste approach, the frequent use of factual data and the baring of devices, as taboo. He argued that such methods encouraged fragmentary, subjective attitudes towards the world. Fatalism and irrationality would follow and contribute to the ultimate irrationality – Fascism.

Lukács made a case for the continuing relevance of the nineteenth-century Realist novel. He believed that novelists like Balzac and Tolstoy clearly revealed the connections that made up the societies in which they lived. Therefore, whatever their personal politics, they had played a progressive role. Adapting their methods to modern circumstances was, for Lukács, the most responsible way in which an author could contribute to defeating Fascism.

His chief opponent was Brecht. The latter's most critical remarks about Lukács were made in the late thirties, but remained unpublished until 1967, a decade after Brecht's death: a clue to the enormous influence of Lukács on the cultural establishment of the Soviet bloc. Brecht and Lukács were Communists who assumed that Marxism provided the key to understanding and changing the world. In literary matters, they shared a common antipathy to Naturalism, as epitomised by Zola, for its inability to penetrate surface phenomena. But over the politics of Modernism they were divided.

Brecht was much more receptive to the radical possibilities of new media such as film and photography. Like Benjamin, however, his enthusiasm was tempered by scepticism. He disliked most 'New Photographers', who were in his view too interested in lighting and not enough in the significance of the objects photographed. With typical crudity, he mocked their ideas about using the camera to increase popular visual awareness by asking the rhetorical question 'By the way, do you know what the backside of a woman looks like? No, I mean what it really looks like?' In a famous statement, he noted the inability of a photograph of a Krupp steelworks to reveal the exploitation that was going on inside, an attack on photographic Naturalism with which Lukács would have probably agreed. Indeed Lukács frequently attacked literary Naturalism by using the adjective 'photographic' in a pejorative way.

For Brecht the camera's mechanical eye was problematic but fascinating. Film and photography were incorporated into his theatre work and he co-scripted the film *Kuhle Wampe* (1932). This film, named after a colony of unemployed on the outskirts of Berlin, contained many examples of cinematic montage and was probably the nearest film equivalent to Heartfield's work. (One sequence juxtaposed the working-class father Bönike engrossed in reading aloud a newspaper account of the exploits of the German spy and *femme fatale* Mata Hari, and the less exotic scene of his wife trying to sort out household bills.) During the Second World War Brecht collected press

Greater London Council hoarding
1984

photographs from newspapers and magazines and added four-line verses, creating what he called 'photo epigrams'. These were published in 1955 as the *Kriegsfiebel* (War Primer), edited and introduced by his collaborator Ruth Berlau. In her introduction she compared photographs to hieroglyphs, and saw Brecht's experiments as aids to their decipherment. Brecht was also a great admirer of Heartfield's use of photographs. They did theatre work together in the twenties and again in the fifties. When Heartfield was snubbed by the GDR authorities, Brecht was his staunch defender, offering him work and nominating him for membership of the Academy of Arts.

In his attacks on Lukács, Brecht never discussed photomontage, but he provided arguments which could be used to defend Heartfield's work. Like Lukács, Brecht wanted to encourage types of art which permitted audiences critically to understand the world, but he refused to accept that this could be done by merely updating Balzac. For Brecht, the Realism of an artwork was not assessed by comparing it with the products of nineteenth-century novelists: 'Were we to copy the style of these Realists, we would no longer be Realists'. He described as Realist any work, however experimental, which helped audiences to grasp reality. In this sense, Heartfield was a Realist since his art helped people understand and oppose the Fascist nightmare.

Even by the early thirties the technique was widespread. In 1931 an international exhibition was held in Berlin showing the use of photomontage in art, advertising and political propaganda. Today photomontage is a commonplace, especially in commercial art. Fifty years after Heartfield, can photomontage still stimulate critical thought?

Klaus Staeck has tried to deal with this question. In West Germany where almost every home has a video recorder Staeck is aware of the radical potential of new media, and particularly of video. But he believes that, paradoxically, a saturation of moving pictures has created an increased desire for the static image. In an afterword to a recent West German paperback of Heartfield's work Staeck warned that slavish imitation of Heartfield will turn a revolutionary technique into a mere convention but at the same time he stressed that Heartfield's methods — the use of the photograph as a didactic weapon and the use of the most advanced technology to reach a mass audience — still have relevance in today's radically different circumstances. Hence the title of his afterword, quoting Heartfield's 1937 essay on Daumier — 'As Alive as Ever'.

John Heartfield

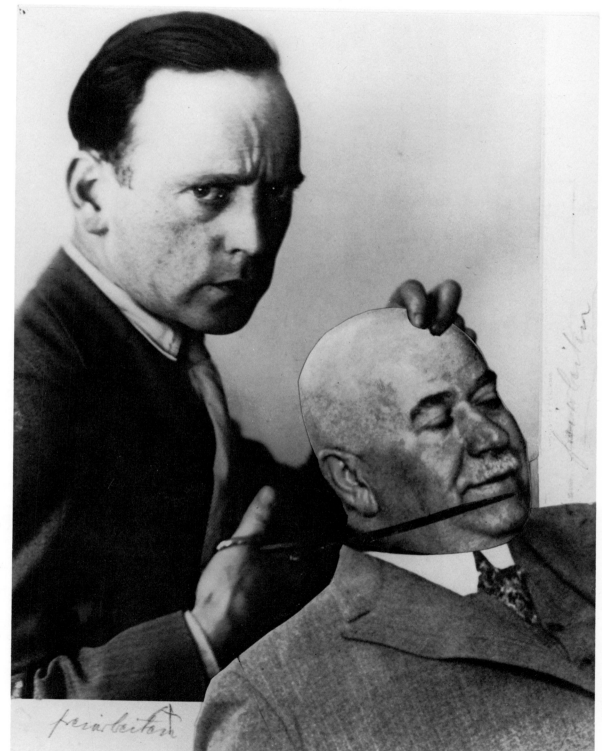

Heartfield und Polizeipräsident Zörgiebel
Benütze Foto als Waffe
[Heartfield and police president Zörgiebel
Use photography as a weapon]
A-I-Z, vol XVIII, no 37, in a review of the 'Große Berliner Kunstausstellung', 1929

This montage shows the artist removing the head of Zörgiebel, the Berlin Chief of Police, held responsible by Communists for the killing of May Day demonstrators in 1929.

SLIDE / PHOTOCOPY

Nach zehn Jahren: Väter und Söhne 1924
[After ten years: fathers and sons 1924]
1924

This montage was generally considered the first example of Heartfield's more mature satirical work. According to Wieland Herzfelde, the enlarged montage was part of a window display in the Malik Verlag bookshop. It was surrounded by ration books, photographs of the tennis-playing crown prince, newspaper pages listing the names of the war dead and other documents relating to World War I.

Several artists commemorated the tenth anniversary of the beginning of World War I and warned against a renewed danger from chauvinists and militarists: Frans Masereel produced his 'Political Drawings against the War'; Ernst Friedrich's multilingual photo-text book 'War against War' was published; Otto Dix produced fifty etchings for the cycle 'War'.

Heartfield's montage was first published in *AIZ* ten years later, with the title *After twenty years!*, [*AIZ*, vol XIII, no 37, 1934].

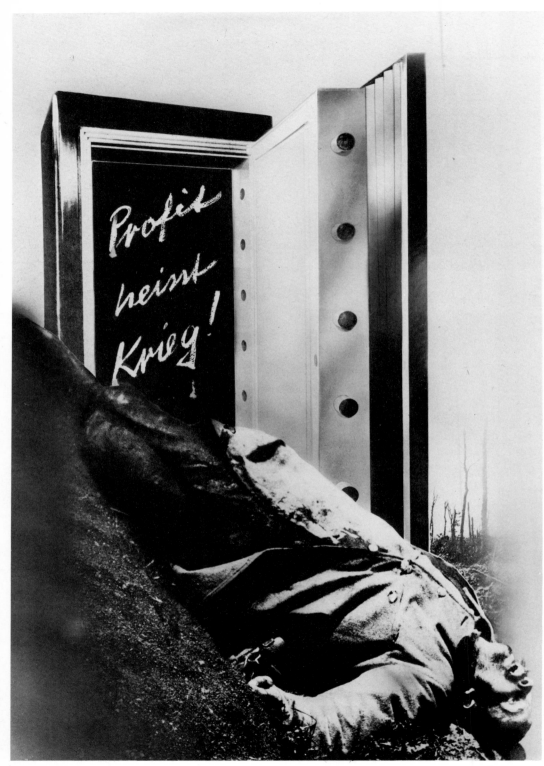

Profit heißt Krieg
[Profit means war]
Cover of the pamphlet *13 Jahre Mord*,
(13 years of Murder), 1927

The link between profiteering and
war was a familiar theme of the left
in the twenties.

Zwangslieferantin von Menschenmaterial – Nur Mut! Der Staat braucht Arbeitslose und Soldaten!
[Forced supplier of human ammunition – Take courage! The state needs unemployed and soldiers!]
A-I-Z, vol IX, no 10, 1930

Heartfield's montage seems almost prophetic: the National Socialists later encouraged women to lead a life revolving around the '3 Ks': *Kinder, Küche, Kirche* (children, kitchen, church). Motherhood was encouraged with rhetorical, institutional and financial means. The Nazis also awarded a golden Mother's Cross for having produced eight children, a silver one for six and a bronze one for four.

The montage was later republished by Wieland Herzfelde with the title '*Ihr Mütter, lasset eure Kinder leben!*' (Mothers, let your children live!), a line from a Brecht poem.

△

Gespensterstunde
[Ghost hour]
1930
Probably unpublished

Rendezvous of reactionaries in a Berlin cemetery.

▷

Zum Krisen-Parteitag der SPD
[On the occasion of the crisis party conference of the
Social Democratic Party]
Subtitle: Vets in Leipzig (= SPD): obviously we are
going to draw the tiger's teeth (capitalism), but we have
to make him better and stronger first.
A-I-Z, vol X, no 24, 1931

One of Heartfield's anti-Social Democratic Party
montages; in the Communist view, the Social Democrats
were collaborating with the centre-right Brüning
government.

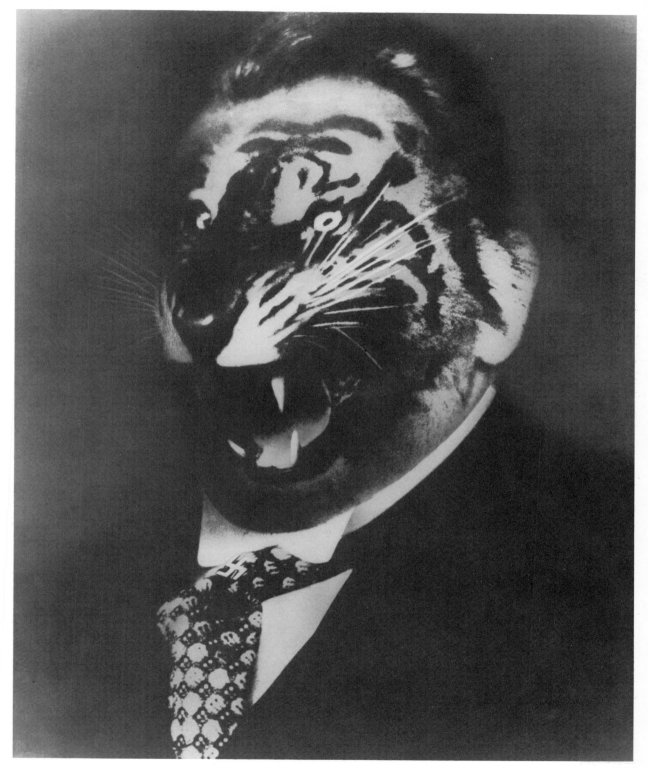

Ab 1. Januar neue Briefmarken im Dritten Reich
[From 1 January new postage stamps in the Third Reich]
On the stamps: *5 Tausend Tote – Dritte Reichspest*
(5 thousand dead – Third Reich plague)
A-I-Z, vol XIII, no 1, 1934

The word 'Reichspest' plays on the similarity between
the German words 'Post' (post) and 'Pest' (plague).

Das tote Parlament [The dead Parliament]
Subtitle: This is what's left of the year 1848!
A-I-Z, vol IX, no 42, 1930

Paragraph 48 of the Weimar Constitution allowed Chancellor
Brüning to rule with emergency powers ignoring Parliament.
1848 was the year of the Frankfurt Parliament; short-lived but
an important landmark in the history of German democracy.

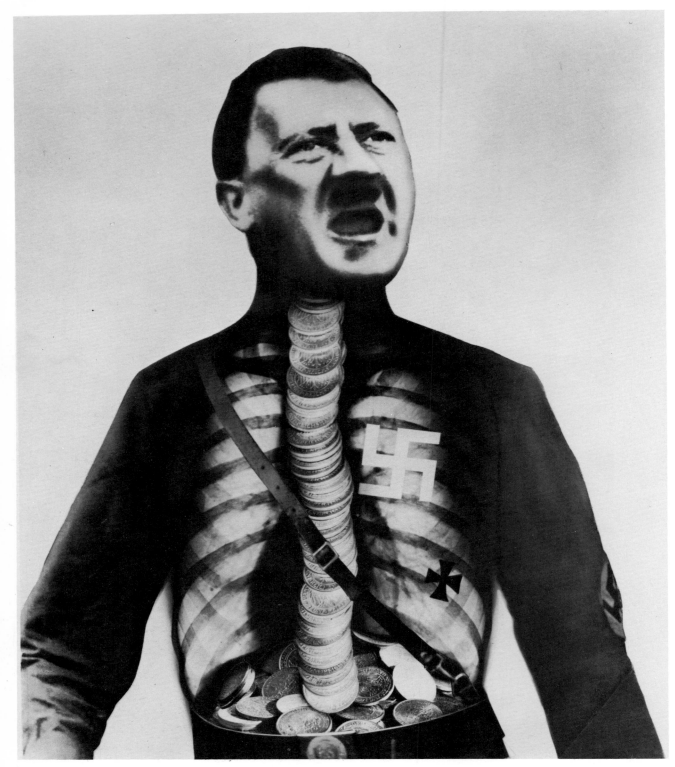

◁

Adolf – der Übermensch.
Schluckt Gold und redet Blech
[Adolf – the Superman.
Swallows gold and spouts
junk]
A-I-Z, vol XI, no 29, 1932

Enlarged versions of this
poster were pasted up all
over Berlin and led to fights
between young Communists
defending the posters and
Nazis who wanted to tear
them down.

▷

Der Sinn des Hitlergrußes:
kleiner Mann bittet um große
Gaben. Motto: Millionen
stehen hinter mir!
[The meaning of the Hitler
salute: little man asks for big
gifts. Motto: millions stand
behind me!]
A-I-Z, vol XI, no 42, 1932

Heartfield reveals that Hitler is
paid by big business and that
the 'millions' referred to in a
Hitler speech are not Hitler's
devoted followers but large
sums of money.

Werkzeug in *Gottes Hand?*
Spielzeug in Thyssens
Hand!
[Tool in God's hand? Toy in
Thyssen's hand!]
AIZ, vol XII, no 31, 1933

Kube, the Supreme President of the Mark Brandenburg and leader of the National Socialist Group in the Prussian Parliament, called Hitler a 'tool in God's hand'. The industrial magnate Fritz Thyssen was the manager of one of the largest trusts in Germany and had just been appointed 'economic dictator' of Germany's most important industrial region, Rhineland-Westphalia. Thyssen had been a friend and financial backer of Hitler and the Nazis from an early time when other capitalists were still keeping their distance.

Heartfield probably got the idea for this montage from a George Grosz drawing, *Stinnes and his President* which shows the industrialist Stinnes with President Ebert as a puppet (in *Abrechnung folgt!*, Malik Verlag, 1925). In both cases the toy is a *Hampelmann* (puppet).

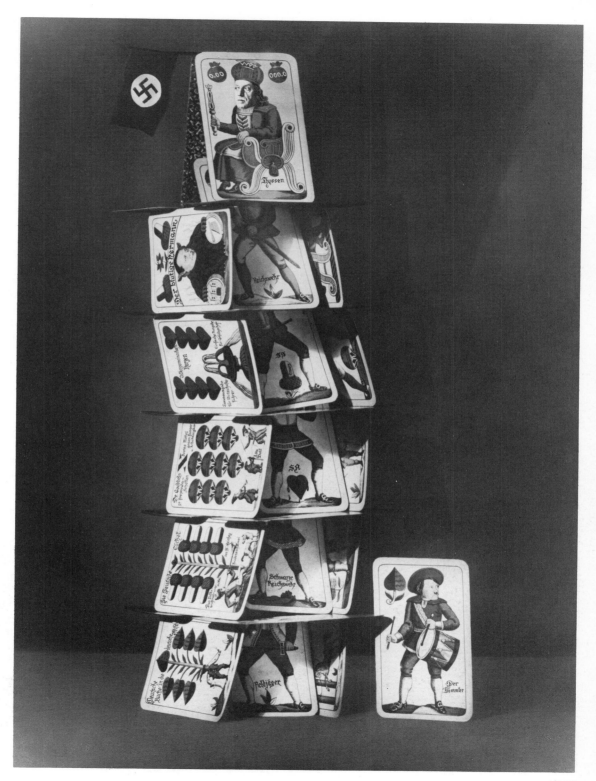

Das tausendjährige Reich
[The thousand-year Reich]
AIZ, vol XIII, no 38, 1934

Heartfield satirises Hitler's
boast that the Third Reich
will last 'a thousand years'
by representing it as an
unstable house of cards.
The industrialist Thyssen is
on the card at the top,
Hitler is the drummer boy
at the bottom, with the
Army, SS, SA, Goering and
Goebbels in between.

◁

Mimikry
[Mimicry]
Subtitle: When all attempts to carry
National Socialist ideas to the work-
ing class failed, Goebbels had one
last desperate idea: he persuaded the
'Führer' to wear a Karl Marx beard
when addressing workers.

Newspaper report of 8 April 1934:
'Beside Goethe's bust and the Eagle
with Swastika, this year's National
Labour Front First of May medal
also shows the Bolshevik symbols of
Hammer and Sickle, apparently in an
effort to win over the workers who
are still in opposition to the regime.'
AIZ, vol XIII, no 16, 1934

▷

*'Spieglein, Spieglein an der
Wand, wer ist der Stärkste im
ganzen Land?' 'Die Krise'*
['Mirror, mirror on the wall,
who is the strongest in the
land?' 'The crisis']
AIZ, vol XII, no 33, 1933

The montage was a response
to the international London
Conference (2 June to 7 July
1933) which failed to reach an
agreement on how to tackle
the world economic crisis.
Text and image refer to the
fairy tale, Snow White and the
Seven Dwarfs.

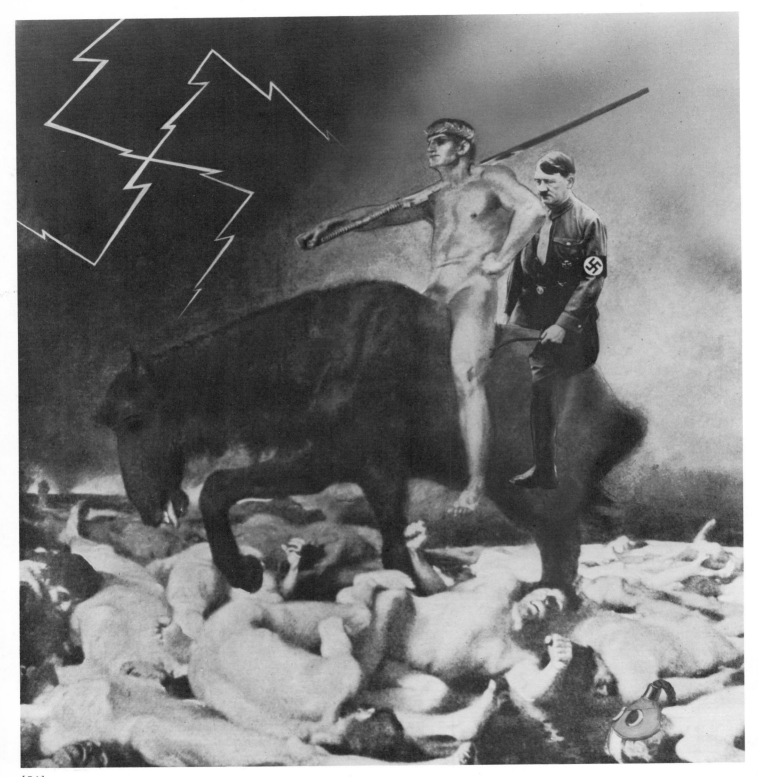

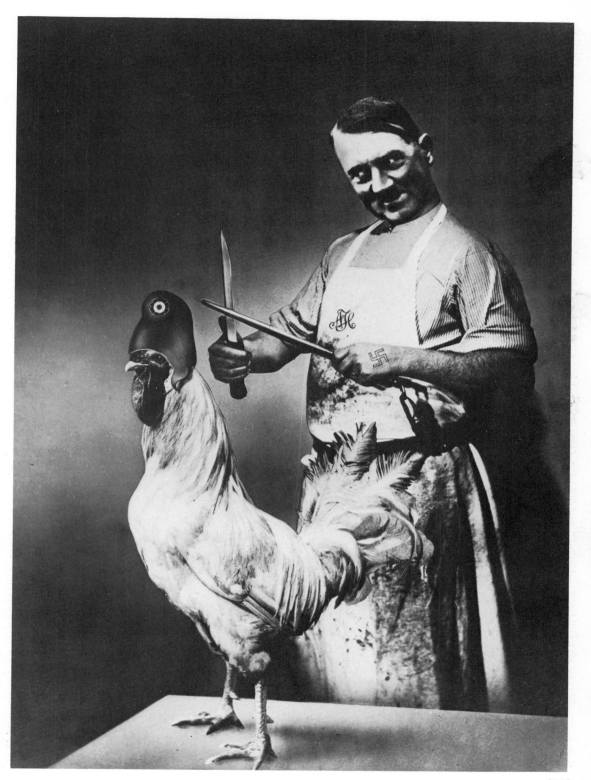

◁

Der Krieg
[War]
Subtitle: A painting by Franz
v. Stuck. Brought up to date
by John Heartfield.
AIZ, vol XII, no 29, 1933

At the 2nd International
Disarmament Conference in
1933, Germany demanded the
expansion of her army from
100,000 to 200,000 soldiers.
The request was rejected.
Germany left the Conference
in October.

▷

*Nur keine Angst – er ist
Vegetarier!*
[Don't worry – he's a
vegetarian!]
Regards, Paris, 7 May 1936

In the original version the
French Foreign Minister Laval
stands on the left and calms
the Gallic rooster, the symbol
of France. In 1939 a new version was published by the
English magazine *Lilliput*, in
which Heartfield replaced
Laval with Bonnet, the new
Foreign Minister. This
example, which omits the
figures of the politicians altogether, is taken from the book
on Heartfield by his brother
Wieland Herzfelde published
in 1962.

◁

*Zur Gründung der
deutschen Staatskirche*
[On the foundation of the
German state church]
Subtitle: The crucifix was
not yet heavy enough
AIZ, vol XII, no 23, 1933

The montage uses
Thorwaldsen's painting of
Christ. Hitler, though a
Catholic himself, reorga-
nised the Protestant
Church in Germany and
installed pro-Fascist clerics
at every level.

▷

*O Tannenbaum im deut-
schen Raum, wie krumm
sind deine Äste!*
[Oh Christmas tree in
German lands, how bent
are your branches!]
AIZ, vol XIII, no 52, 1934

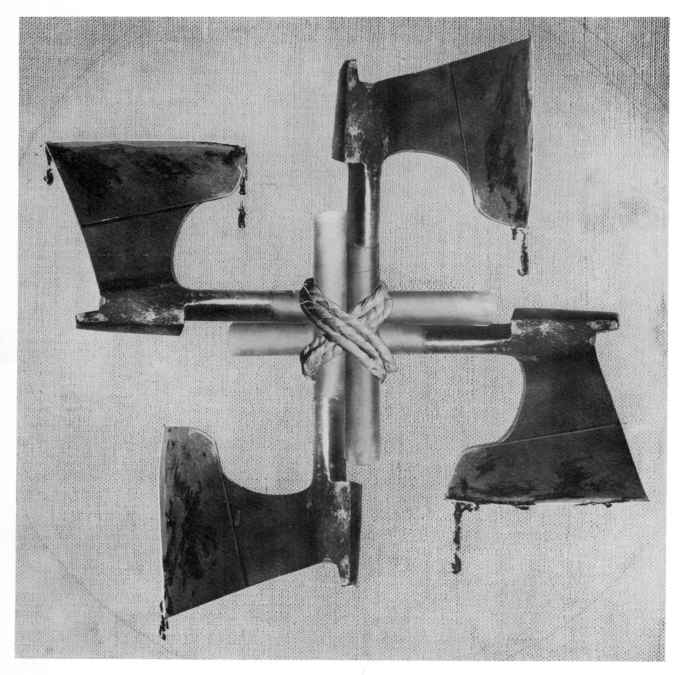

△ *Der alte Wahlspruch im 'neuen' Reich: Blut und Eisen*
[The old slogan in the 'new' Reich: blood and iron]
AIZ, vol XIII, no 10, 1934

'The old slogan' of Bismarck's famous 'blood and iron' speech
of 1886. In 1934 the bloody persecution of all Hitler's enemies
was being intensified.

▷ *Durch Licht zur Nacht* [Through light into the night]
AIZ, vol XII, no 18, 1933

On 10 May 1933, books were being burned in Berlin and in
many other German towns. But in Berlin, Reich Propaganda
Minister Goebbels himself supervised the burning. In the
background the burning Reichstag.

[59]

◁

Goering, der Henker des Dritten Reichs
[Goering, the executioner of the Third Reich]
AIZ, vol XII, no 36, 1933

This montage on the Reichstag fire was also used as the cover of *Braunbuch über Reichstagsbrand und Hitlerterror* (Brown book on the Reichstag fire and the Hitler Terror), a Communist publication in several languages. The Reichstag, the parliamentary building in Berlin and symbol of the Weimar Republic, had been set ablaze on 27 February 1933. The Nazis arrested most Communists and Socialists for their alleged conspiracy to overthrow the state. Emergency laws were introduced the next day.

▷

Zum Brandstifter-Prozeß in Leipzig
[On the occasion of the arson trial in Leipzig]
Subtitle: They twist and turn and call themselves German judges
AIZ, vol XII, no 41, 1933

One of a series of powerful montages against attempts to frame Communists during the Reichstag fire trial. This one was also used as a postcard with the title 'Swastika Vipers'.

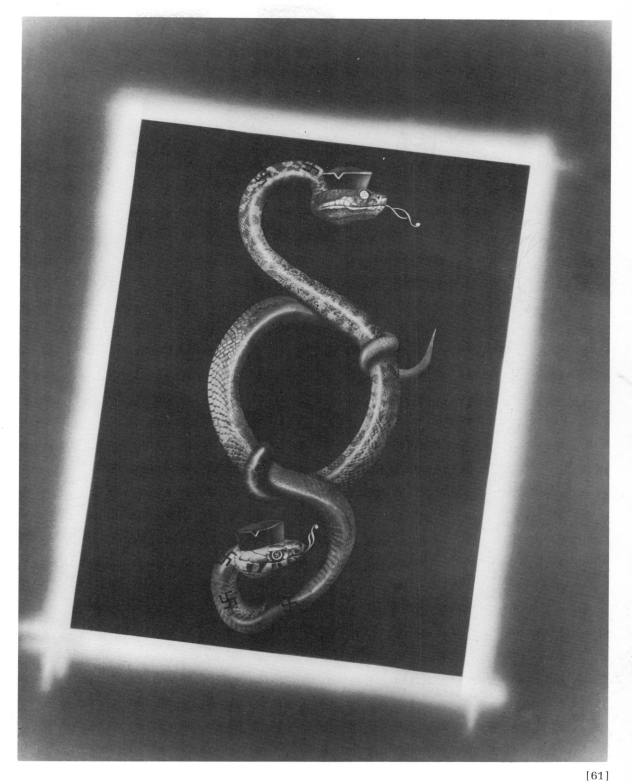

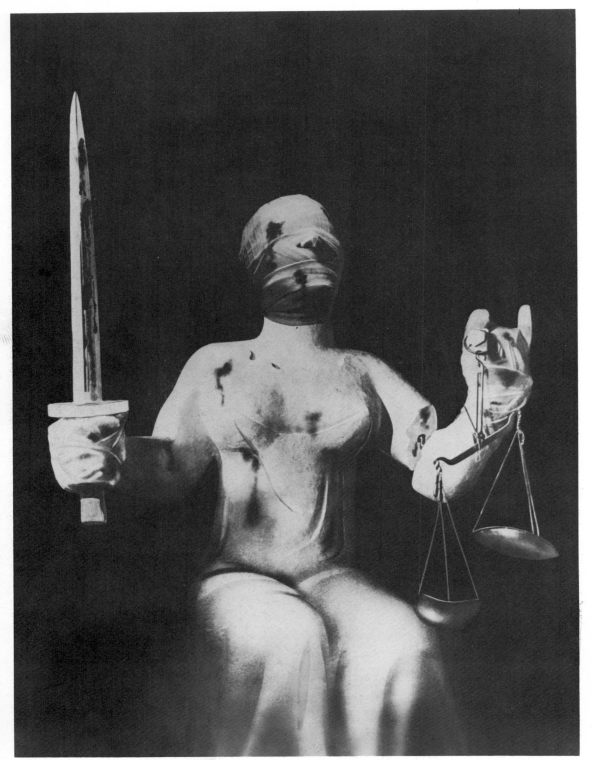

Der Henker und die Gerechtig-
keit. Göring im Reichstags-
brandprozeß: *Für mich ist das
Recht etwas Blutvolles*
[The executioner and Justice.
Goering at the Reichstag fire
trial: For me Justice is a bloody
affair]
AIZ, vol XII, no 47, 1933

Der Richter – Der Gerichtete:
Dimitroff – Ministerpräsident
Göring
[The judge – the judged: Dimitroff
– Minister President Goering]
AIZ, vol XII, no 45, 1933

Five Communists were accused of
arson in the Reichstag fire trial.
One of them, the Bulgarian emigré
Georgi Dimitroff, conducted his
own defence. Radio transmissions
of the trial soon had to be
stopped when the Nazis realised
that Dimitroff would be acquitted
by the jury while Goering risked
being revealed as the true culprit.

Das Spiel der Nazis mit dem Feuer. 'Wenn die Welt erst brennt, werden wir schon beweisen, daß Moskau der Brandstifter war.'
[The Nazis' play with fire. 'When the world is burning, we shall easily prove that Moscow was the incendiary.']
AIZ, vol XIV, no 9, 1935

Goering burns the globe with his torch. This montage commemorates the second anniversary of the burning of the Reichstag and the ensuing anti-Communist witch hunt.

Der friedfertige Raubfisch
[The peaceful fish of prey]
Subtitle: 'I detest collective
security! I invite all the
small fish to enter into
bilateral treaties with me.'
VI, no 19, 1937

Hitler preferred bilateral to
multilateral treaties, the
most famous one being the
Nazi-Soviet Non-Agression
Pact of 1939. The montage
with its theme of 'big fish
eat little fish' is evocative of
drawings by both Bosch
and Bruegel. The body is
Goering's (see *The Nazis'
play with fire*).

John Heartfield

Zur Intervention des Dritten Reichs.
Je mehr Bilder sie weghängen, um so
sichtbarer wird die Wirklichkeit!
[On the intervention of the Third
Reich. The more pictures they
remove, the more visible the reality
will be!]
AIZ, vol XIII, no 18, 1934

Montage referring to the Mánes
caricature exhibition held in Prague
in 1934 and the German Embassy's
protest at some of the exhibits.
(See pages 9–10)

Lenins Vision ward Wirklichkeit
[Lenin's vision became reality]
AIZ, vol XIII, no 21, 1934

An example of Heartfield's pro-Soviet montages: it was made to celebrate the production of the 100,000th tractor in Stalingrad. Lenin had spoken of '100,000 first-class tractors by the year 1919', but didn't really believe that this was achievable.

◁

Alle Fäuste zu einer geballt
[Every fist clenched into
one]
AIZ, vol XIII, no 40, 1934

A montage in support of
the call for an anti-Fascist
United Front in the League
of Nations plebiscite in
January 1935 which was to
prevent the Saarland,
administered by the League
from 1919 to 1935, from
being swallowed up by
Fascist Germany. The plebiscite resulted in its restor-
ation to Germany.

▷

*Die Freiheit selbst kämpft
in ihren Reihen*
[Liberty herself fights in
their ranks]
VI, no 1, 1936

On 17 July 1936 war broke
out between the Spanish
government and the armies
of Generals Franco, de
Llano and Mola who were
supported by Fascist
Germany and Italy. Only
after a two-year siege were
the Fascists able to take
Madrid. The montage
combines Delacroix's
Liberty Guiding the People,
1831, with a press photo-
graph of the defence of
Madrid.

Photomontage after Heartfield

MICHAEL BENNETT
United Kingdom

The Dung Market
1984

Illustration for William Morris's utopian novel
News from Nowhere, used in the 'William Morris
Today' exhibition by the Institute for Contemporary Arts, London. 1984 was the 150th anniversary of the birth of William Morris.

MICHAEL BENNETT
Stop and Search
Published as a Christmas card for the
National Council for Civil Liberties,
1981

The British police have the
right to stop and search people
if they have reasonable
grounds for suspecting that
the person concerned may be
carrying drugs, firearms, documents relating to terrorism or
(in some places) stolen goods.
In practice, these police
powers often get abused, and
the National Council for Civil
Liberties campaigns to make
people aware of their rights.
The NCCL is the largest independent organisation working
to protect and extend civil
rights in the UK.

◁

MICHAEL BENNETT

Bombing begins in Five Minutes

New Society, 1984

A 'joke' by President Reagan who made this
reference to a nuclear attack on the Soviet Union,
when testing the microphones before a radio
broadcast. When the 'joke' was also transmitted
on the radio, it caused outrage around the world.

▷

MICHAEL BENNETT

Dirty Ronnie

New Statesman, 13 March 1981

Both title and image refer to the film
'Dirty Harry' with Clint Eastwood as
a self-righteous cop who takes the
law into his own hands.

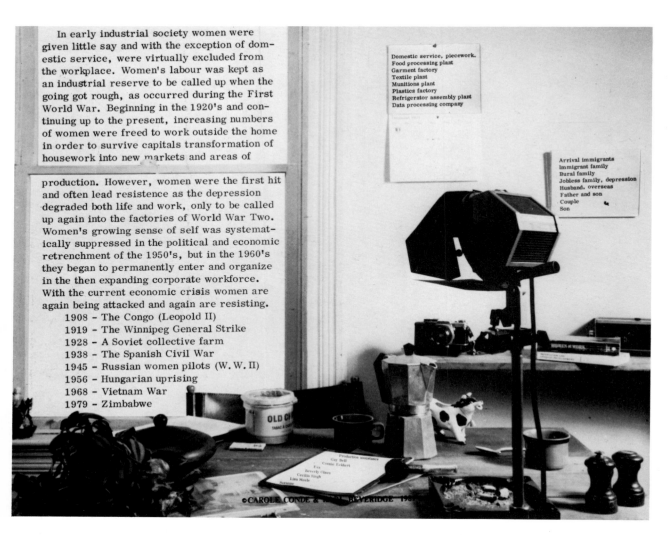

In early industrial society women were given little say and with the exception of domestic service, were virtually excluded from the workplace. Women's labour was kept as an industrial reserve to be called up when the going got rough, as occurred during the First World War. Beginning in the 1920's and continuing up to the present, increasing numbers of women were freed to work outside the home in order to survive capitals transformation of housework into new markets and areas of production. However, women were the first hit and often lead resistence as the depression degraded both life and work, only to be called up again into the factories of World War Two. Women's growing sense of self was systematically suppressed in the political and economic retrenchment of the 1950's, but in the 1960's they began to permanently enter and organize in the then expanding corporate workforce. With the current economic crisis women are again being attacked and again are resisting.

1908 – The Congo (Leopold II)
1919 – The Winnipeg General Strike
1928 – A Soviet collective farm
1938 – The Spanish Civil War
1945 – Russian women pilots (W.W.II)
1956 – Hungarian uprising
1968 – Vietnam War
1979 – Zimbabwe

Domestic service, piecework.
Food processing plant
Garment factory
Textile plant
Munitions plant
Plastics factory
Refrigerator assembly plant
Data processing company

Arrival immigrants
Immigrant family
Rural family
Jobless family, depression
Husband, overseas
Father and son
Couple
Son

©CAROLE CONDÉ & KARL BEVERIDGE 198

CAROL CONDÉ
AND
KARL
BEVERIDGE
Canada

Work in Progress
1982

Full caption
on page 78

ON PAGES 76 AND 77 CAROL CONDÉ AND KARL BEVERIDGE

Condé and Beveridge have described their overall aim as 'visualising the past'. *Work in Progress* is a sequence of nine colour photomontages which attempts to convey the recent history of Canadian women. The significance of the home setting has been explained by the artists:

> The choice of domestic setting in *Work in Progress* rather than that of a workplace is to anchor the dominant material and ideological role assigned to women. Even though women have entered paid labour, they must still perform the unpaid labour of housework in their 'spare time', and it is still the home that provides the ideological framework within which women are seen to function.

The window in each montage contains a picture of the contemporary world usually showing women's involvement in Socialist history. The company calendar on the wall shows the jobs open to Canadian women at the time, and the photograph nearby represents the changing family. The first montage includes text which briefly introduces the series and lists the inset photographs. Its similarity to film credits emphasises the connection between a photomontage series like this and film.

Work in Progress has been exhibited in North America, Australia and the UK but, as well as showing work in conventional art galleries and magazines Condé and Beveridge frequently collaborate with labour organisations and use their specialised outlets.

DAAR *Operatie? Over je auto heb je nog meer te zeggen*
[Operation? You have more say in what happens to your car]

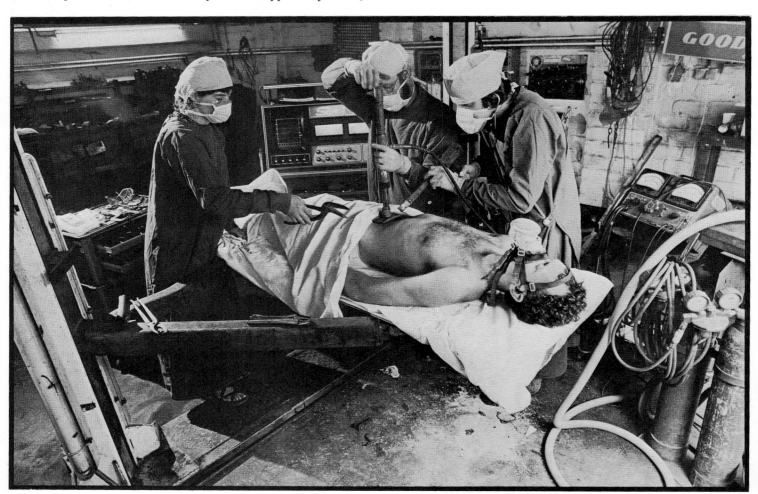

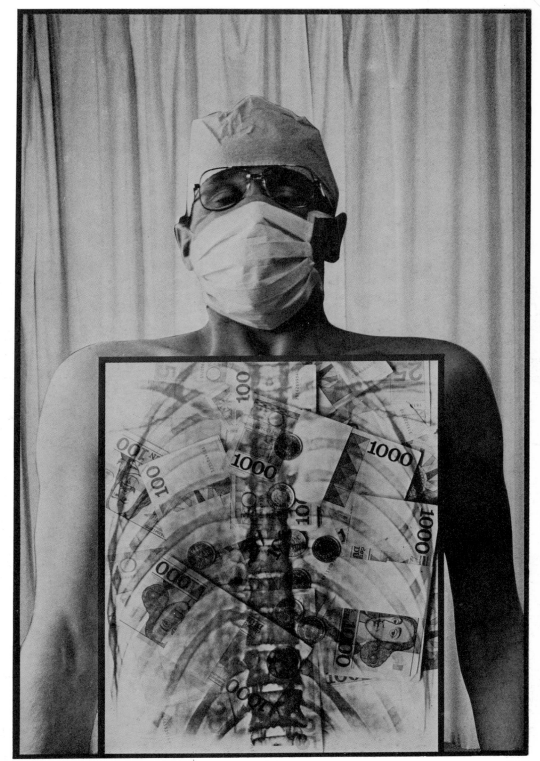

DAAR (Paul Kooijman and Hans Zoete)
Discussie Affiches Alledaagse Realiteit
[Posters to provoke discussion about
everyday living]
The Netherlands

All the montages shown here are from the series,
1980–1983

*Gezondheidszorg. Wie wordt er beter
van?*
[Health service. Who profits?]

The use of an X-ray photograph and
money is similar to Heartfield's montage
*Adolf – the Superman. Swallows gold
and spouts junk.* Here the X-ray
photograph reveals the inside of the
doctor rather than the patient.

DAAR
Woonomgeving? Jiff helpt niet tegen gif
[A living environment? Jiff (a window cleaning product) doesn't help against poison]

The dangers of housing people in polluted areas near factories.

DAAR

Voor (huis)vrouwen. Heb je daar nou voor geleerd?
[For (house)wives. Is this what you studied for?]

A degree certificate hangs on the washing line.

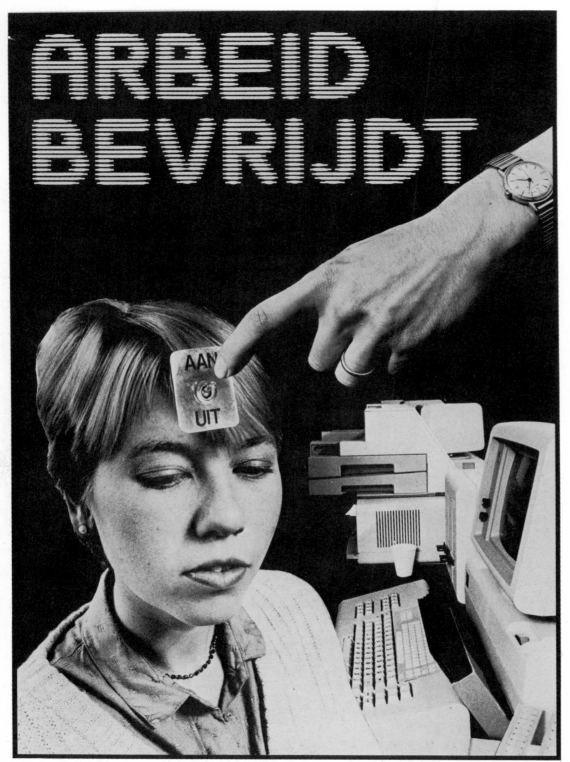

ARBEID BEVRIJDT

DAAR
Werk (-loosheid). Arbeid bevrijdt
[(Un-)employment. Work liberates]

New technology means job losses
for many people and the division
of labour often results in
degrading and tedious work. The
words on the button 'aan-uit' are
'on-off'.

[93]

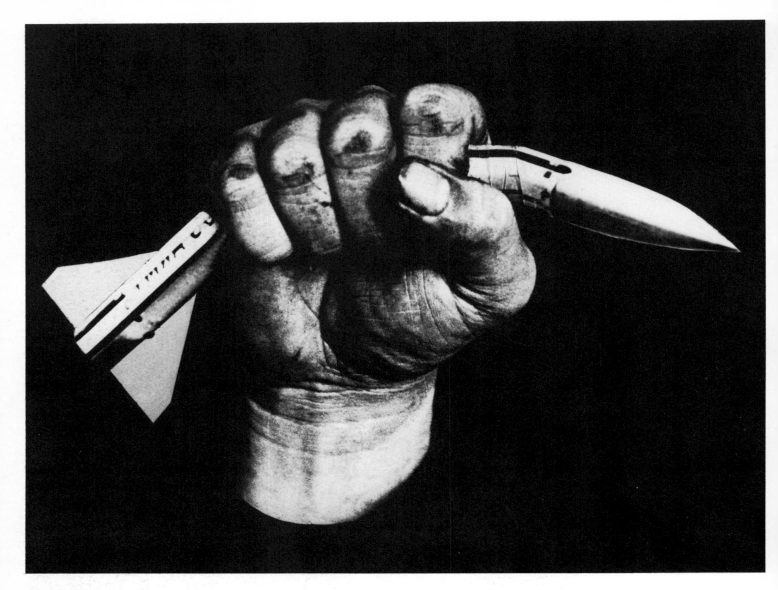

PETER KENNARD
Crushed Cruise
1981

This montage, produced for the Labour Party, was immediately taken up by peace groups around the country and used on badges, banners etc. The hand crushing a missile evokes the Anarchist symbol of hands breaking a rifle.

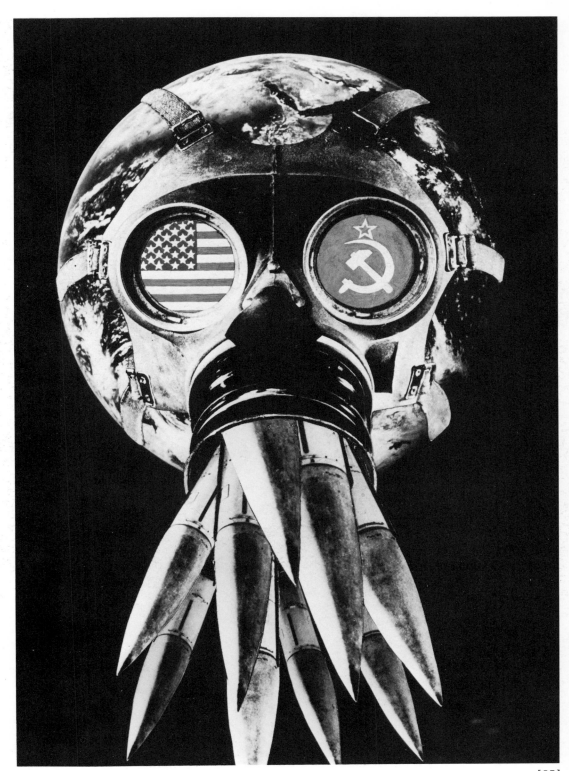

PETER KENNARD
Defended to Death

Cover montage of *Defended to Death. A
study of the nuclear arms race from the
Cambridge University Disarmament
Seminar.* Edited by Gwyn Prins. Penguin
Books, 1983

Kennard attacks the nuclear
policies of both superpowers; an
attitude that forms a clear
contrast with that of the
pro-Soviet Heartfield.

[95]

PETER KENNARD
Hiroshima – CND

Originally published in a poster pack, *CND Picture Show*, by Ed Barber and Peter Kennard, 1982

In the top left corner is a photograph of a watch which stopped at the moment of impact when the bomb fell on Hiroshima. Kennard shows its evolution into a positive image, the symbol for the Campaign for Nuclear Disarmament.

▷

PETER KENNARD
Tanks into Ploughshares

Produced for an educational display pack, *The Socially Useful Show*, published by the Centre of Alternative Industrial and Technological Systems (CAITS), 1982

The display pack aimed at promoting the ideas of the Lucas Aerospace Combine Shop Stewards Committee about the conversion of arms industries to peaceful production.

PETER KENNARD
Falklands commemorative medal
Produced for a GLC booklet, *Jobs for a change*, 1983

The ship is the HMS Antelope going down (according to the *Daily Mail*, 26 May 1982) 'in a blaze of glory', during the Falklands conflict between Britain and Argentina in 1982.

PETER KENNARD
Maggie Regina
First published by the *New Statesman*, front cover 27 May 1983

The portrait of Queen Victoria is taken from the *Illustrated London News*, but Queen Victoria's head has been replaced by that of Margaret Thatcher, who had been calling for a return to 'Victorian values' (hard work, duty, self-reliance). The montage was reprinted in *Time* (20 June 1983) when Thatcher was re-elected.

◁

PETER KENNARD
News Editing on Northern Ireland

Produced for the booklet *The British Media and Ireland*, published by Information on Ireland, 1979

A comment on the established media's attitude to reporting the British military presence in Northern Ireland. The accompanying text, a quote from a BBC TV news sub-editor, reinforces the message: 'I've always assumed the official line is we put the army's version first and then any other'.

▷

PETER KENNARD
Disappeared Prisoners – Chile

Part of the travelling exhibition 'A Documentary on Chile', first shown at the Camerawork Gallery in East London, 1978

The photographs on the wall show Chileans who have been detained by the military intelligence service while the authorities deny any knowledge of their whereabouts. Their pictures are removed by a paint brush.

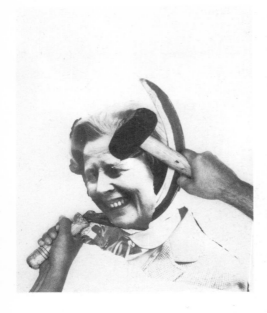

DAVID KING
United Kingdom
A Short Sharp Shock
1980

Used as publicity for Howard Brenton's play of the same title at the Royal Court Theatre, London. The Conservative Arts Minister at the time described the montage as 'deplorable'.

RHINOCEROS
United Kingdom

Peace Game
1983

The title refers to the propaganda film *The Peace Game* made by the British government to present nuclear defence as an effective deterrent and to counter the film *The War Game* made by Peter Watkins and widely used by the Campaign for Nuclear Disarmament.

RHINOCEROS
London Pageantry
1983

A combination of a tourist postcard called 'London Pageantry' and a press photograph
of police in riot gear.

KLAUS STAECK
West Germany

Weinschwemme. Europa ist mehr als die Weinschwemme
[Wine lake. Europe is more than the wine lake]
1984

The wine bottle has been montaged into Bruegel's painting *Tower of Babel* (c.1563). Both montages on this page are a comment on the European Economic Community's agricultural policy and the gluts of produce it causes. For example, by 1991 60 million tonnes of unwanted cereals is expected to flood warehouses throughout the Community.

KLAUS STAECK

Butterberg. Europa ist mehr als der Butterberg
[Butter mountain. Europe is more than the butter mountain]
1984

A packet of German butter has been montaged into a detail of Bruegel's painting *The Wedding Feast* (c.1568).

[104]

Die Null-Lösung

Ich bin der geistige Führer in diesem unserem krisengeschüttelten Land

KLAUS STAECK

Nullösung. Die Null-Lösung
[Zero option. The Zero-option]
1983

The photograph shows the leader of the Conservatives and Chancellor of West Germany, Helmut Kohl. The 'Zero option' refers to a defence policy, popular among conservative politicians of the West, which aims at preserving the current American supremacy in the balance of weapons between the superpowers. But the title also means the Chancellor who is himself a 'zero option' for Germany; a blank, a nonentity.

KLAUS STAECK

Birne. Ich bin der geistige Führer in diesem unserem krisengeschüttelten Land
[Pear. I am the intellectual leader in this our crisis-shaken country]
1982

'Pear' is a colloquial expression in Germany for 'head' and a rotting pear obviously refers to someone stupid. The second part of the caption mimics the ungrammatical and antiquated style of speech used by Chancellor Helmut Kohl. Staeck is also making an allusion to Philipon's portrayal of King Louis Philippe as a pear in his famous caricature of 1831.

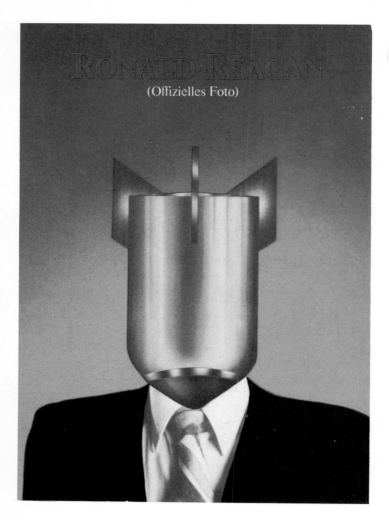

KLAUS STAECK

86 *Ronald. Ronald Reagan (Offizielles Foto)*
[Ronald. Ronald Reagan (official photograph)]
1983

KLAUS STAECK
Fremdarbeiter
[Foreign worker]
1974

The dustman in the foreground wears a star similar to the Star of David Jewish citizens had to wear in the Third Reich. The star is coloured like the Italian flag – red, white and green.

Like many Western countries, West Germany had a shortage of workers in the prosperous fifties and invited 'guestworkers' to fill jobs, especially the more menial ones such as refuse collection. The first wave of immigrant workers came from the Mediterranean countries, especially Italy. Staeck places German hostility to Italians side by side with the anti-Semitism of the Third Reich. A later version of this montage replaces the Italian flag-star with the Turkish flag, referring to the second wave of immigrant workers who now bear the main brunt of xenophobia in Germany.

KLAUS STAECK
Mittelpunkt. Im Mittelpunkt steht immer der Mensch
[Centre. The individual is always at the centre of things]
1981

Bar codes are just one example of today's increasing
computerisation but Staeck makes them stand for all the
information hoarded by authorities and institutions and also for the
ever-encroaching threat this represents to our liberty.

KLAUS STAECK
Mona Lisa. Niemand ist vollkommen
[Mona Lisa. Nobody is perfect]
1981

Staeck's contribution to the 'Year of the Disabled'.

KLAUS STAECK

Weltregierung. Zur Erinnerung an die Vereidigung der neuen Weltregierung

[World government. In memory of the swearing in of the new world government]

1981

The power of multi-nationals. Staeck uses as examples all the major oil companies.

KLAUS STAECK

Pharmaindustrie. Wir stoßen uns an Ihren Krankheiten gesund. Ihre Pharmaindustrie

[Pharmaceutical industry. We are getting well on your diseases. Yours sincerely, pharmaceutical industry]

1981

KLAUS STAECK
For wider streets – Vote Conservative
1974

This postcard was produced to coincide with the exhibition 'Art into Society – Society into Art' held at the Institute of Contemporary Arts in London in 1974, the year of two general elections in Britain. The exhibition, part of a 'German month' organised by the Goethe Institute in London, was intended to give an overview of current art in West Germany with particular emphasis on artists who tried to relate their art to society's problems. German conservatives protested at the 'one-sidedness' of the exhibition.

KLAUS STAECK
Übergewicht. Jeder 2. Deutsche hat Übergewicht
[Overweight. One in two Germans is overweight]
1977

The border outline of the card is printed in the colours of the West German flag – black, red and gold.

KLAUS STAECK

Direkte Werbung I
[Direct Advertising I]
1970

One of a series of montages published in Staeck's book, *Pornografie* (1971), which contains — contrary to all expectations — an attack on advertising techniques. Staeck uses the image or slogan of the original advertisement, but makes the brutality of this kind of marketing directly visible.

KLAUS STAECK

Heidelberg. Besucht das schöne Heidelberg — bekannt für seine Straßen und Plätze
[Heidelberg. Visit beautiful Heidelberg — famous for its streets and squares]
1975

Staeck has used a poster issued by the Heidelberg tourist office and montaged a new photograph into the frame. Instead of a view from the 'Philosophers' Path', he shows the demolition of an old philosopher's house (Kuno Fischer) in the name of modern town planning and land speculation. Staeck produced 3,000 of these posters and had them pasted up all over Frankfurt on hoardings and in underground stations.

KLAUS STAECK
*Goethe. 225 Jahre Goethe. 111 Jahre
Farbwerke Hoechst*
[Goethe. 225 years of Goethe. 111 years
of Chemical Industries Hoechst]
1974

The original painting is Tischbein's
portrait *Goethe in the Roman
Campagna* (1786). This had been
montaged into the skyline of Goethe's
birthplace, Frankfurt, to make an
official tourist poster and postcard on
the occasion of his 225th anniversary
(1974). The original title of the poster
and card was '225 years Goethe': Staeck
added '111 years Chemical Industries
Hoechst'; provided a greenish hue for
the sky, and gave Goethe a skeletal leg
to dangle in the River Main — all of
which is an attack on the air and water
pollution caused by Hoechst.

IKARUS made in USA

ROLF STAECK
East Germany

Ikarus made in USA
1980

Rolf Staeck makes the point that American foreign policy causes
soldiers to die, but others are profiting from it. The montage is
also an allusion to Heartfield's *Do you want to fall again so that
shares can rise?* (1932) which shows a dying soldier clutching
his shoulder about to fall, against a background of shares from
the leading industrialists.

CATH TATE
United Kingdom

Prevent Street Crime

Produced as a poster, postcard, T-shirt, on a mug and in a calendar, 1982

The slogan is taken from a campaign by the London Metropolitan Police warning the public against street crime. At the same time the Prime Minister Margaret Thatcher was beginning to cut the funds for the inner cities.

[114]

CHRISTER
THEMPTANDER
Sweden

John Wayne, Supermaskulinen
[John Wayne, super-masculine]

Published in *Klipp Till* and widely used
in the United States, 1973

John Wayne, the super-
masculine hero of many
Westerns (Masculinity = War?)
actively supported the US war
effort in Vietnam.

CHRISTER THEMPTANDER
Vi glömmer aldrig Wounded Knee
[We'll never forget Wounded Knee]

Published in *Klipp Till* and as postcard, stickers and posters. Widely distributed in the United States, 1971

The title refers to the Massacre of Wounded Knee (1890) in which over 200 Sioux men, women and children were killed by US troops. For the Indian liberation groups that have been active in the United States since the sixties, this incident, which concluded the conquest of the American Indian, has achieved a symbolic status.

[115]

CHRISTER THEMPTANDER   *Vad händer i Kreml?*
                        [What's happening in the Kremlin?]
                        Published as a postcard, 1981

Themptander rejects the Soviet version
of Communism as a model for a
democratic Socialist society.

CHRISTER THEMPTANDER
General Jaruzelski
Published as a demonstration poster/banner, originally in full colour, 1981/82

On 13 December 1981 General Jaruzelski introduced martial law
and ended the Polish experiment with democracy and all
concessions won by the independent trade union movement
Solidarity. Thousands of political and trade union figures were
detained, including the Solidarity leader Lech Walesa.

CHRISTER THEMPTANDER
Peace Dove – Military Recipe 1983
Full-colour postcard, 1983

Themptander refurbishes the exhausted symbol of the 'Peace Dove'.

RONALD "RIOT" REAGAN: WAR AGAINST POVERTY

CHRISTER THEMPTANDER
Ronald 'Riot' Reagan
Subtitle: War against Poverty
Published as a postcard, 1982

The destruction of American inner city
areas by Reagan's monetarist policies.

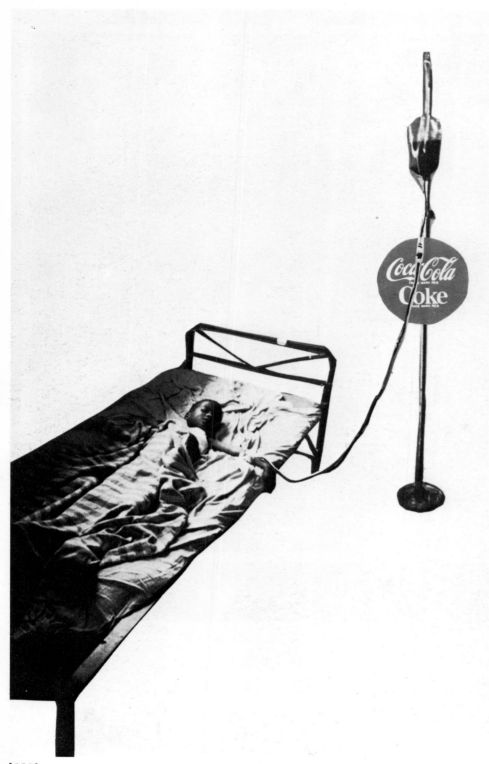

CHRISTER THEMPTANDER
Coca Cola det hör till
[Coke – it's the real thing]

Published in *Klipp Till* and as exhibition poster and demonstration banner, 1971

American economic imperialism: in this case the international marketing of Coca Cola in the Third World while children are starving or need medical attention. The title is Coca Cola's own advertising slogan.

CHRISTER THEMPTANDER
End white rule in black South Africa
1984

Portrait of P. W. Botha, Prime
Minister and leader of the white
minority government in South Africa.
Despite increased international
protests and trade boycotts the
South African government sticks to
its Apartheid politics.

CHRISTER THEMPTANDER
Three montages from his book, *Våra vanligaste Övermän*
[Our most common top dogs – in revealing close-ups]
Arbetarkultur/Bildförlaget öppna ögon, 1981
Also published as postcards

In these grotesque photomontages the figures are not identifiable as specific individuals. Instead Themptander is making a series of general statements about capitalism and patriarchy.

CHRISTER THEMPTANDER
Annupå fri fot...
[Still on the loose...]
1984
[124]

Still on the loose: capitalists who profit from factories which emit dangerous chemicals and are responsible for the death of forests, the poisoning of lakes.

Sources

GENERAL

Ades, Dawn, *Photomontage*, London, Thames and Hudson, 1976
Aragon, Louis, *Les Collages*, [reprint of 1935 edition], Paris, Hermann, 1965
Diederich, Reiner and Grübling, Richard, *"Unter die Schere mit den Geiern!" Politische Fotomontage in der Bundesrepublik und Westberlin*, West Berlin, Elefanten Press Verlag, 1977
Digby, John and Digby, Joan, *The Collage Handbook*, London, Thames and Hudson, 1985
Evans, David and Gohl, Sylvia, 'The Political Art of Photomontage', *New Socialist* (UK), no. 15, Jan.-Feb. 1984, pp. 40–4
Jürgens-Kirchhoff, Annegret, *Technik und Tendenz der Montage in der bildenden Kunst des 20. Jahrhunderts*, Gießen, Anabas-Verlag, 1978
Patti, Giuliano, Sacconi, Licinio and Ziliani, Giovanni, *Fotomontaggio – Storia, tecnica ed estetica*, Milano, Gabriele Mazzotta editore, 1979
Sobieszek, Robert A., 'Composite Imagery and the Origins of Photomontage', *Artforum* (USA), vol 17, part 1, Sept. 1978, pp. 58–65 and part 2, Oct. 1978, pp. 40–5
Wescher, Herta, *Die Geschichte der Collage*, Köln, Verlag M. DuMont Schauberg, 1968
Worpole, Ken, 'Do you ever wish you were better informed?', *New Statesman* (UK), 19–26 Dec. 1980, pp. 34–5

HEARTFIELD

BOOKS AND ARTICLES

Deutsche Akademie der Künste, *John Heartfield – photomontages*, London, Arts Council of Great Britain, 1969
Fredriksson, Inger, *Konsten spränger ramarna, John Heartfield och det politiska fotomontaget*, Stockholm, Akademilitteratur, 1979
Heartfield, John, *Krieg im Frieden – Fotomontagen zur Zeit 1930–1938*, München, Carl Hanser Verlag, 1972; Frankfurt am Main, Fischer Taschenbuch Verlag, 1982; English edition:
John Heartfield: Photomontages of the Nazi Period, London, Gordon Fraser and Universe Books, 1977
Herzfelde, Wieland, *John Heartfield – Leben und Werk*, Dresden, VEB Verlag der Kunst, 1962
Hölterhoff, Manuel, 'Heartfield's Contempt', *Artforum* (USA), vol 15, part 3, Nov. 1976, pp. 58–65
März, Roland (ed.), *John Heartfield – Der Schnitt entlang der Zeit (Selbstzeugnisse, Erinnerungen, Interpretationen)*, Dresden, VEB Verlag der Kunst, 1981
John Heartfield, Der Sinn von Genf: Wo das Kapital lebt, kann der Friede nicht leben! 1932, East Berlin, Staatliche Museen zu Berlin/ Nationalgalerie, 1981
Siepmann, Eckhard, *Montage: John Heartfield, Vom Club Dada zur Arbeiter-Illustrierte-Zeitung*, West Berlin, Elefanten Press Verlag, 1977
Spence, Jo, 'The sign as a site of class struggle – Reflections on works by John Heartfield', *Block* (UK), no. 5, 1981, pp. 2–13

Töteberg, Michael, *Heartfield – In Selbstzeugnissen und Bilddokumenten*, Reinbek bei Hamburg, Rowohlt Taschenbuch Verlag, 1978
Tucholsky, Kurt, *Deutschland, Deutschland über alles. Ein Bilderbuch von Kurt Tucholsky und vielen Fotografen, montiert von John Heartfield*, [facsimile of 1929 edition] Reinbek bei Hamburg, Rowohlt Verlag, 1973

FILM

Herbst, Helmut, *John Heartfield, Fotomonteur*, 35 mm, 65 mins., Cinegrafik, 1977

BERMAN

Berman, Mieczyslaw, *Fotomontaggi/Photomontages*, Milano, Galleria Schwarz, 1973
Czartoryska, Ursula, 'Photomontage in Poland', *Creative Camera* (UK), no. 163, Jan. 1978

RENAU

Renau, José, *fata morgana USA*, East Berlin, Eulenspiegel Verlag, 1967
Renau catalogue, València, Galeria Punto, 1977

SHITOMIRSKY

Shitomirsky, Alexander, *Political Photomontage*, (Russian text), Moscow, Plakat, 1983

CONDÉ/BEVERIDGE

Fleming, Martha, 'The Production of Meaning', *Block* (UK), no. 8, 1983, pp. 24–38
Weber, John, 'Narrative Dimensions in North American Photography', *European Photography*, no. 24, Oct.–Dec. 1985

DAAR

Arian, Max and van Schaik, Pim, 'Die Platen zeggen precies wat je denkt', Een boekje over acht series Diskussie Affiches Alledaagse Realiteit van Paul Kooijman en Hans Zoete, Rijswijk, Ministerie van Welzijn, Volksgezondheid en Cultuur, 1984

DUNN/LEESON

'The Changing Picture', *Photography/Politics 2*, London, Comedia, 1986
'The Changing Picture of Docklands', in Kahn, Douglas and Neumaier, Diana (eds.), *Cultures in Contention*, Seattle, Real Comet Press, 1985

Dunn, Peter and Leeson, Loraine, 'The Fire and the Fireplace', *Block* (UK), no. 1, pp. 15–33, 1979
'Work in Progress: an interview with Peter Dunn and Loraine Leeson', *Camerawork* (UK), no. 21

HOLTFRETER

Holtfreter, Jürgen, *Politische Fotomontage*, West Berlin, Elefanten Press Verlag, 1979

KENNARD

BOOKS AND ARTICLES

Berger, John, 'Seeing through lies', *Sanity* (UK), Dec.–Jan. 1981–2, p. 14
Cork, Richard, 'Danger Signs', *The Listener* (UK), 8 August 1985
Kennard, Peter, *Target London*, [set of photomontages], London, GLC, 1985
Kennard, Peter and Sissons, Ric, *No Nuclear Weapons*, London, CND/Pluto Press, 1981
Pollitt, Nigel, 'Who is this chap Kennard?–Interview', *The Leveller* (UK), 7–20 Aug. 1981, pp. 8–9
Tisdall, Caroline and Kennard, Peter, 'Peter Kennard', *Art and Artists* (UK), Dec. 1973

VIDEO

Rodrigues, Chris and Stoneman, Rod (dirs.), *Photomontage Today: Peter Kennard*, 35 mins, London, Arts Council of Great Britain, 1983

STAECK

Art into Society – Society into Art, Seven German Artists, exhibition catalogue, London, ICA, 1974, pp. 87–94
Coutts-Smith, Kenneth, 'The Political Art of Klaus Staeck', *praxis* (USA), no. 4, 1978, pp. 13–55
Evans, David and Gohl, Sylvia, 'Political Photomontage – Heartfield to Staeck', *Camerawork* (UK), no. 20, pp. 6–7
Karst, Ingeborg (ed.), *Der Fall Staeck oder wie politisch darf die Kunst sein?*, Göttingen, Verlag Gerhard Steidl, 1975
Jappe, Georg, 'Klaus Staeck – interview', *Studio International* (UK), Mar. 1976, pp. 137–40
Staeck, Klaus, *Die Kunst findet nicht im Saale statt, Politische Plakate*, Reinbek bei Hamburg, Rowohlt Verlag, 1976
Die Reichen müssen noch reicher werden, Politische Plakate, Reinbek bei Hamburg, Rowohlt Taschenbuch Verlag, 1973
staeckbrief, [newsletter and catalogue], Edition Staeck, Postfach 10 20 63, Ingrimstraße 3, D-6900 Heidelberg 1, West Germany, Tel: (06221) 247 53.

THEMPTANDER

Fredriksson, Inger and Themptander, Christer, *Amerikana – I odjurets buk*, Lund, Bo Cavefors Bokförlag, 1976

'The Image as Weapon: An Interview with Christer Themptander', praxis (USA), no. 4, 1978, pp. 56–68

Themptander, Christer, Klipp till, Politiska Fotomontage, Stockholm, Arbetarkultur, 1980
Våra vanligaste Övermän, Stockholm, Arbetarkultur/Bildförlaget öppna ögon, 1981

DADA

Ades, Dawn, Dada and Surrealism Reviewed, London, Arts Council of Great Britain, 1978

Haenlein, Carl-Albrecht (ed.), Dada – Photographie und Photocollage, Hannover, Kestner Gesellschaft, 1979

Willett, John, The New Sobriety, Art and Politics in the Weimar Period 1917–33, London, Thames and Hudson, 1978
The Weimar Years. A culture cut short, London, Thames and Hudson, 1984

PRODUCTIVISM

Arvatov, Boris, Kunst und Produktion, München, Carl Hanser Verlag, 1972

Benjamin, Walter, 'The Author as Producer' (1934), Understanding Brecht, London, NLB/Verso, 1977

Bojko, Szymon, New Graphic Design in Revolutionary Russia, London, Lund Humphries, 1972

Gaßner, Hubertus and Gillen, Eckhart, Zwischen Revolutionskunst und Sozialistischem Realismus, Köln, DuMont, 1979

Karginov, German, Rodchenko, London, Thames and Hudson, 1979

Knödler-Bunte, Eberhard and Erler, Gernot (eds.), Kultur und Kulturrevolution in der Sowjetunion, West Berlin, Ästhetik und Kommunikation Verlag, 1978

Lissitzky-Küppers, Sophie, El Lissitzky, London, Thames and Hudson, 1968

Lodder, Christina, Russian Constructivism, New Haven and London, Yale University Press, 1983

Tretjakow, Sergei, Lyrik Dramatik Prosa, Leipzig, Reclam, 1972

AGITPROP

'Der Arbeiter-Fotograf (and The British Worker in Photographs 1839–1939)', Creative Camera (UK), nos. 197–8, May-June 1981

Boehncke, Heiner, Gorsen, Peter and Knödler-Bunte, Eberhard (eds.), 'Arbeiter-Illustrierte-Zeitung, Eine Dokumentation zur "A-I-z" und zum "Arbeiter-Fotografen"', Ästhetik und Kommunikation, no. 10, Jan. 1973, Reinbek bei Hamburg, Rowohlt Verlag

Evans, David and Gohl, Sylvia, 'AIZ – A Marxist-Leninist Picture Magazine', Camerawork (UK), no. 25, Nov. 1982

Gross, Babette, Willi Münzenberg: A Political Biography, Michigan State University Press, 1974

Ricke, Gabriele, Die Arbeiter-Illustrierte-Zeitung, Hannover, Internationalismus Verlag, 1974

Surmann, Rolf, Die Münzenberg-Legende. Zur Publizistik der revolutionären Arbeiterbewegung 1921–1933. Köln, Prometh Verlag, 1984

Verband Arbeiterfotografie (ed.), Arbeiterfotografie, West Berlin, Elefanten Press Verlag, 1978

Weber, Richard and others (eds.), Der Arbeiter-Fotograf, Dokumente und Beiträge zur Arbeiterfotografie 1926–1932, Köln, Prometheus Verlag, 1977

Willmann, Heinz, Geschichte der Arbeiter-Illustrierte-Zeitung 1921–1938, East Berlin, Dietz Verlag, 1975

PHOTOGRAPHY

Benjamin, Walter, 'A Small History of Photography (1931)', One Way Street and other writings, London, NLB/Verso, 1979

Dennett, Terry, Evans, David, Gohl, Sylvia and Spence, Jo, (eds.), Photography/Politics: One, London, Photography Workshop, 1979

Eskildsen, Ute, 'Photography and the Neue Sachlichkeit movement', Neue Sachlichkeit and German Realism of the Twenties, London, Arts Council of Great Britain, 1978

Eskildsen, Ute and Horak, Jan-Christopher (eds.), Film und Foto der zwanziger Jahre. Eine Betrachtung der Internationalen Werkbundausstellung "Film und Foto" 1929, Stuttgart, Württembergischer Kunstverein, 1979

Gräff, Werner, Es kommt der neue Fotograf!, [facsimile of 1929 edition] Köln, Verlag der Buchhandlung Walther König, 1978

Mellor, David (ed.), Germany, The New Photography 1927–33, London, Arts Council of Great Britain, 1978

Roh, Franz and Tschichold, Jan (eds.), foto-auge/oeil et photo/photo eye, Stuttgart, Wedekind, 1929

Stotz, Gustaf et al, Film und Foto, [facsimile of 1929 edition], New York, Arno Press, 1979

Vierhuff, Hans Gotthard, Die Neue Sachlichkeit, Malerei und Fotografie, Köln, DuMont Buchverlag, 1980

POLITICAL CARTOONS

Bann, Stephen, 'Cartoons, Art and Politics', Getting them in Line. An Exhibition of Caricature in Cartoon, Canterbury, Centre for the Study of Cartoons and Caricature, University of Kent, 1975

Benjamin, Walter, 'Eduard Fuchs, Collector and Historian' (1937), One Way Street and other Writings, London, NLB/Verso, 1979

Gombrich, E.H., 'The Cartoonist's Armoury', Meditations on a Hobby Horse, Oxford, Phaidon Press, 1963

Gombrich, E.H., and Kris, E., Caricature, Harmondsworth, Penguin, 1940

Grosz, George, A Small Yes and A Big No. The Autobiography of George Grosz, London, Allison & Busby, 1982 [first published under the title Ein kleines Ja und ein großes Nein, Reinbek bei Hamburg, Rowohlt Verlag, 1955]
The Day of Reckoning, [reprint of 1925 edition], London, Allison & Busby, 1984
The Face of the Ruling Class, [reprint of 1921 edition], London, Allison & Busby, 1984

März, Roland, Daumier and Heartfield – Politische Satire im Dialog, East Berlin, Staatliche Museen zu Berlin/Nationalgalerie, 1981

Schneede, Uwe M., George Grosz, His life and work, London, Gordon Fraser, 1979 [first published, Stuttgart, Verlag Gerd Hatje, 1975]

Zeman, Zbyněk, Heckling Hitler, Caricatures of the Third Reich, London, Orbis, 1984

REVOLUTIONARY AESTHETICS

Berger, John, 'The Political Uses of Photomontage', Selected Essays and Articles, Harmondsworth, Penguin, 1972

Brecht, Bertolt, Kriegsfiebel, East Berlin, Eulenspiegel Verlag, 1955
Kuhle Wampe. Protokoll des Films und Materialien, Frankfurt am Main, Suhrkamp, 1969
Über die bildenden Künste, Frankfurt am Main, Suhrkamp, 1983

Eagleton, Terry, Marxism and Literary Criticism, London, Methuen, 1976
Walter Benjamin or Towards a Revolutionary Criticism, London, NLB/Verso, 1981

Jameson, Fredric (ed.) Aesthetics and Politics, London, NLB/Verso, 1977

Lunn, Eugene, Marxism and Modernism. An Historical Study of Lukács, Brecht, Benjamin and Adorno, London, NLB/Verso, 1985

Staeck, Klaus, 'Lebendig wie nie. Ein Nachwort', John Heartfield, Krieg im Frieden, Frankfurt am Main, Fischer Verlag, 1981

Willett, John, 'Brecht and the Visual Arts', Brecht in Context, London, Methuen, 1984

Index

Numbers in italics refer to illustrations

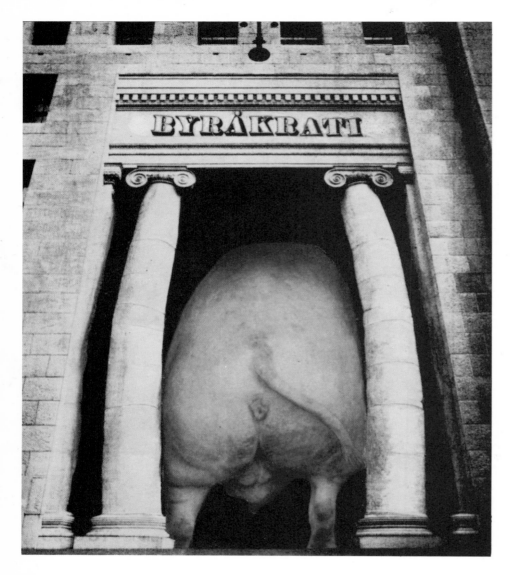

CHRISTER THEMPTANDER
Byråkrati
[Bureaucracy]

Published in *Klipp Till*,
and as a postcard and poster, 1977